AVOCA

café cookbook 2

Editor Hugo Arnold   **Design** Vanessa Courtier   **Copy Editor** Lewis Esson   **Production** Tim Chester

Text © 2002 Hugo Arnold   Photography © 2002 Georgia Glynn Smith

The rights of Hugo Arnold to be identified as the Author of this Work has been asserted by him in accordance with the Copyright, Designs and Patents Act 1988   First published in 2002 by Avoca Handweavers Ltd, Kimacanogue, Co Wicklow. Reprinted 2003 (twice), 2004, 2005 (twice), 2006

Printed and bound in Hong Kong by South Sea International Press

Cataloguing-in-publication Data: a catalogue record for this book is available from the British Library   **ISBN: 0-9538152-1-8**

AVOCA
café cookbook 2

written by Hugo Arnold with Leylie Hayes

photography by Georgia Glynn Smith

CONTENTS

Recipes throughout serve four, unless otherwise stated
Salt and pepper are not listed in the ingredients, but are used extensively
Metric measurements are used as standard

INTRODUCTION

A big thank you to all our customers and to everyone who bought the first Avoca Café Cookbook.

No one was more surprised than we were with its success. It was conceived as a way to set out the Avoca story and pass on some of our most-requested recipes. As with most things at Avoca, we worked hard to do it as well as possible. We would have been pleased to sell ten thousand copies. In the event the Avoca Café Cookbook became an Irish best seller with over 60,000 copies sold. Indeed, it is selling still.

For us, though, a more fulfilling sign of its success comes late in the day – literally. Pick up the phone after hours in our offices and chances are it's someone with a question about the Cookbook. 'I don't have that ingredient, will this do instead?' 'I'm not sure how to do this, can you help?' That people were obviously using it and interested enough to call us encouraged us to consider a follow-up volume. We were not, however, interested in doing another book for the sake of it. The Avoca Café Cookbook 2 had to be bigger and even better than its predecessor.

In the intervening two years, the Café and Foodhall at our Suffolk Street shop have opened and the menus in our other kitchens have developed and expanded. So we had hundreds of new recipes, new ideas and new favourites.

The food in the cafés is not overly complicated. It is good honest food produced with passion and attention to detail. More than ever we have a reinforced sense of the critical importance of fresh good ingredients. Quality in, quality out. We have always strived to source the least processed, best raw materials.

Perhaps above all, however, we insist on freshness. Organic is great, but if it has travelled half way around the world there is no point in that. So an emphasis on quality and local sourcing became a corner-stone of this second book.

We have questioned, cooked, discussed and trawled until we were happy that Cookbook 2 would deliver even more recipes and more practical advice. We hope what follows will become a dog-eared favourite like it's predecessor in kitchens everywhere.

Thanks again for all your support. Good cooking.

Simon Pratt

MENU PLANNING

Regardless of whether it is dinner for two, an impromptu supper for friends or a large feast, the menu is crucial. This is the driving force, the one item that guides you through the shopping, the sea of mess you are about to create in your kitchen, allows you to maintain your sanity when you cannot quite see the wood from the trees.

Time for this planning phase is crucial. It is rarely something to be achieved in minutes on a Saturday morning as you juggle writing a menu with the knowledge that as you write and try to think, the car parks are filling up with shoppers. Allow yourself some space and treat this part of the process with the same importance as the cooking.

The key objective when writing a menu is to achieve balance. As people eat they experience a number of different sensations – sight, taste and texture, to name just three - and your menu has to guide them through these so they move seamlessly but with a sense of adventure from one to another. Put a plate of salad in front of someone and invariably they are assailed by bright colours, crunchy textures and sweet vegetable flavours; perhaps peppery radishes, sweet salad leaves and smooth, unctuous olive oil.

The following few pages highlight the key elements in writing a menu and make suggestions of dishes from the book, as well as pointing out occasions when buying some Parma ham, smoked salmon, or even a fruit tart can make your event more successful and less stressful. We are, after all, trying to celebrate and enjoy, not get stressed out and exhausted.

Seasonality   The key to all good menus is seasonality. This is not as straightforward as it once was. What, after all, is seasonal? Come June, we expect to be eating tomatoes, but there is no way we can buy Irish tomatoes that taste of anything in June, we still have our summer to come.

You need to interpret to some degree, but tomatoes from Italy in June are far more seasonal than strawberries from Argentina in December. The seasonality issue also rests on expectation. If your guests expect to see a winter stew in November, it is probably with good reason. Hold on the asparagus until June.

Clashes   An ingredient should only ever figure once in a meal. Thus if you start with the potato pancake, smoked salmon and crème fraîche on page 57, you do not then have potatoes in your main course. This rule becomes more complicated if you are having a buffet for example, when ingredients like tomatoes, roasted red peppers and black olives can easily end up in a number of dishes. The reason is twofold. Firstly, it creates boredom in the eyes of the diner and, secondly, likes and dislikes come into play. If one of your guests is not crazy about tomatoes, and two or three dishes contain tomatoes, it cuts down their options.

Cooking techniques   Don't make things difficult for yourself. If your main course is complicated and involves last-minute preparations, do a first course that is simple and probably cold. If you are going to have a roast as your main course, don't also roast your starter. If the dessert is going to be a tart, don't also serve up beef Wellington – too much pastry is definitely a bad thing.

Bread   This is a vital ingredient to the success of any meal. It must be a rustic, well-made and deliver some bite and satisfaction. It is easy to serve too much bread at the start; people are hungry and inclined to eat too much of it.

First courses   The role of this course is to awaken and energize your guests. Colour is enormously helpful here and the Americans tend with good reason towards salads, a lesson we would do well to follow. Keep things light, bright and simple, even in winter. Roasted roots – for example carrots or beetroots – can look incredibly refreshing, even on a bitterly cold day.

Soup   In the cafés, customers often opt for soup and a salad, so our soups tend to be warming and filling. This makes them more suited to a lunch than as the first course to a large meal. Some of the soups – for example the Ham hock and split pea soup with mint relish on page 29 or the Seafood chowder on page 21 – can form the central course of an informal supper. Followed by cheese and salad, they may break the meat-and-two-veg rule, but then we are less inclined to eat like that any more.

Tarts   Tarts to start, tarts to main course, tarts to finish. In the cafés, we make an awful lot of tarts, some of which are gloriously simple, like the Chocolate tart on page 125, while others are slight twists on much-loved themes, like Crab, coriander and chilli tart, page 115. These savoury tarts can form the centrepiece of a light lunch or informal supper, but again are not designed as a first course unless perhaps served in small portions with a green salad alongside.

Main courses   Many people are often concerned with whether they are serving enough food. The main course is where much of the attention lies and consequently rather a lot of the volume. When was the last time you came home from somebody's house feeling hungry? Think about what has come before and what is to follow. If you've started with the Thai chicken salad on page 88, for example – which has quite a complex range of flavours – then your main course should be fairly simple and straightforward; the Chilli bean bake on page 142, for example, or the Grilled sea bass, spinach and chickpea pilaf and raita on page 160.

Stay away from cheese if you are going to serve cheese later and think about your dessert. If it is the Bread and butter pudding, page 219, your main course should be very simple and quite light.

Salads   The French serve salad after the cheese with good reason and the Italians finish up with salad for the same reason, they refresh. Most of the salads in this book are composed salads involving more ingredients than salad leaves, the idea being to eat them on their own as a first course, perhaps, or with a bowl of soup as a meal. Simple salads, made up of leaves – either mixed or a single variety of lettuce – and dressed with a simple vinaigrette are hugely refreshing and often welcome after a main course.

Cheese   We are often asked about how to put together a good cheese board. The two rules are to offer variety, both in taste and texture, and not to over-supply. Six or seven cheeses on a board may be ideal for a French restaurant trying to impress, but you would be well advised to concentrate on buying three cheeses in excellent condition, one hard, one soft and one blue.

Desserts   The object here is to provide an end, a full-stop. What you want to avoid however, is the idea of being stuffed. A dessert that rounds things off so you feel just tempted enough will leave your guests getting up from the table thanking you rather than cursing their own greed.

Sugar is a tricky ingredient and needs to be handled carefully. The objective is to provide a contrast with the savoury and salty dishes that have gone before. You also need to provide change, which is one reason why some of the best desserts are ice-cold. It is a refreshing shock to the system.

Wine   Wine is not referred to throughout the rest of the book, but most of us drink wine when we eat, almost certainly these days when we entertain. Pairing food and wine is a massive subject and well beyond the scope of this book.

It is a common approach to look at the prime ingredient and pair accordingly. Thus beef goes with claret, salmon goes with some crisp unoaked white from the New World. The trouble comes when you start adding other ingredients, the Parma wrapped fillet of lamb with Savoy cabbage on page 185 is a fairly complicated dish and cabbage is a devil to partner with wine. Claret would be wiped away, far better to go for an earthy Rhone. You need to look at the dish as a whole.

Secondly, take guidance, if you can, from the region that inspires the dish. The Confit of duck salad on page 85 draws its inspiration from south-west France and the wines of that region – big, tannic and earthy – are the ones to source for this dish.

You   In all this, the one vital ingredient missing is the cook. What do you feel like cooking? What inspires you? The list above is a guide, but don't underestimate the vital role that you play in all this. There is huge choice available to every cook and half the battle is in trying to reduce the choice down.

In books, this is often expressed as a need to go to the shop or market and see what is good. The down side of this approach is you are then faced with writing your menu as you shop and many of us don't want to do that. Which brings us neatly back to seasonality. If you keep within the seasons, you are unlikely to go too far wrong. You need to want to cook whatever you have chosen, that soul is vital.

A menu for two

starters
Pea, pancetta and broad bean salad   *page 98*

main course
Seared tuna with tomato, caper and avocado relish
page 171
Steamed new potatoes
dessert
Summer fruit tartlets   *page 123*

A buffet feast

Anti pasti plate (a selection of cured meats, farm-house cheeses and char-grilled/marinated vegetables)
Gazpacho   *page 17*
Duck terrine   *page 50*
Pastrami salmon *page 169*
Baked red peppers with tomatoes, mozzarella and anchovies   *page 38*
Spiced cannellini beans and tomato salad   *page 83*
Thai chicken salad   *page 88*
Crispy smoked bacon, gently sautéd leeks and mature cheddar quiche   *page 110*
A tossed green salad
A basket of warm bread

Chocolate tart   *page 125*
Mixed berry terrine   *page 216*

A menu for six

starters
Prawns pil pil   *page 54*

main course
Chicken and veal cannelloni   *page 196*
A tossed green salad

dessert
Raspberry and hazelnut meringue   *page 212*

A menu for sixteen

starters
Mezze plate   *page 45*

main course
Duck shepherd's pie   *page 200*
A tossed green salad

dessert
Lavender and rosemary roasted plums   *page 220*

SOUPS

When is soup a soup? When is it a meal? When is it a snack? A light broth – with some vegetables or fish, chicken or beef – can become a meal in moments, particularly when teamed with noodles, rice or pasta. Thick and creamy vegetable soups are also quick and easy to make and surpass even the most elaborate of shop-bought versions. Build your soup up with relishes and salads and what may once have been humble will be transformed into something quite grand indeed.

Ingredients must be of the best quality; this is no place for limp and tired vegetables. It is worth remembering, however, that winter vegetables in particular will keep happily for days in a cool vegetable rack – think cabbages, squashes and the likes of carrots and turnips.

Our modern magpie approach to cooking allows us to scan the world for ideas and inspiration, be that sweet-and-sour soups from the East, the gentle use of herbs and spices from the Middle East, as well as our own native concentration on basic good-quality ingredients – from squeaky leeks to dark and forbidding beetroot, from lush and vibrantly green peas to blush-red tomatoes. What more honest food is there?

Gazpacho

In Spain, in the height of the summer, this soup is served in shallow bowls with ice-cubes, a refreshing start to any meal. It is usually garnished with more cucumber, freshly diced tomato and red onion and sometimes croutons. You might also want to think about basil leaves and black olives.

2 slices of stale bread
4 tablespoons olive oil
about 2 tablespoons red wine vinegar
1 cucumber
1 red pepper
1 green pepper
1 red onion
2 x 400g tins of chopped tomatoes
3 garlic cloves

Soak the bread in the olive oil and 1 tablespoon of red wine vinegar for 30 minutes.

Roughly dice all the vegetables, reserving a few for garnishing. Combine the tinned tomatoes, bread, vegetables and garlic and blitz to a purée. Season with salt and pepper and red wine vinegar to taste. Serve with a few of the reserved diced vegetables. If you like the idea of an extra kick, some finely sliced red chilli can be added at this stage.

Variations   if you want a bit more body in this soup, try gently simmering a chilli or two in the oil. Discard the chilli and proceed with the oil.

Using gelatine, this mixture can be set in glasses, ramekin dishes or a ring mould. For 600ml soup you'll need 1 teaspoon powdered gelatine. Mix this initially with 2 tablespoons of soup in a bowl over a saucepan of simmering water. Pour some more of the cold soup into the gelatine mix, stirring well, and then fold this back into the remaining soup. Lightly grease some cling film with a little oil and line your chosen mould. Pour in the gazpacho mixture and chill until set, about 2 hours. Turn on to a large plate. You can fill the middle with crab or prawn mayonnaise, diced cucumber, or tomato and red onion with coriander and parsley.

Butternut squash soup with garlic croutons

Butternut squash will keep for weeks in a vegetable rack, provided it is dry and cool. For a simple and easy supper, cut one in half, scoop out the seeds and fill each half with cream flavoured with nutmeg, a smashed garlic clove and salt and pepper. Bake in an oven preheated to 180°C/gas mark 4 for 30-40 minutes or until tender. Remove the garlic clove and mash the flesh into the cream as you go.

What follows is a rich and substantial soup, small portions rather than large being the order of the day if you are using it as a starter. If it is for lunch, following it with cheese and salad will be more than sufficient.

1 butternut squash

1 onion

1 potato

1 celery stick

1 carrot

50g butter

1 dessertspoon grated ginger

600ml vegetable stock

4 tablespoons cream or crème fraîche

1 tablespoon finely chopped chives

for the garlic croutons

4 tablespoons olive oil   4 thick slices of bread, crusts removed and cut into 2cm cubes   2 garlic cloves, finely chopped   1 tablespoon finely chopped parsley

Peel the butternut squash, halve it, scoop out the seeds and cut it into 3cm dice. Similarly dice the onion, potato, celery and carrot. Melt the butter on a low heat and gently sauté the onion for 10-15 minutes, stirring occasionally to prevent it catching.

Add the remaining vegetables and cook for a further 2 minutes, stirring so everything is well coated in butter. Add the grated ginger, season with salt and pepper, add the vegetable stock and simmer for 20 minutes, or until the vegetables are soft. Liquidise and check the seasoning.

To make the croutons, heat the olive oil in a frying pan and, when hot, add the cubed bread. Sauté over a medium heat until golden brown. If you are concerned about the amount of oil, you can drain the croutons on kitchen paper at this point. Remove from the heat, add the garlic and parsley and toss in the still-hot pan.

Serve the soup with the garlic croutons, a dollop of cream and some chopped chives.

Roast parsnip soup with apple crisps

Perhaps the sweetest of all the root vegetables, parsnips are an integral part of winter eating, their nutty robust flavour making them as good with roast meats as they are on their own.

3 parsnips, diced
3 tablespoons olive oil
1 onion, finely chopped
1 potato, finely diced
50g butter
600ml light chicken stock
4 teaspoons crème fraîche
4 teaspoons chestnut purée
1 tablespoon snipped chives
for the apple crisps
1 Granny Smith apple or similar

Make the apple crisps well ahead, preheat the oven to 140°C/gas mark 1, core the apple and thinly slice. Lay the slices out on a baking tray and place in the oven for 2 hours, or until dried and crisp.

Preheat the oven to 200°C/gas mark 6. Toss the diced parsnips in the olive oil, season well and roast in the oven for 20 minutes or until well coloured.

Gently sauté the onion and potato in the butter over a low heat for 10 minutes, stirring occasionally. Add the roasted parsnips and the stock and simmer for 20 minutes, or until all the vegetables are soft. Allow to cool slightly, liquidise, then reheat and check the seasoning.

Garnish each bowl with a teaspoon of crème fraîche, a teaspoon of chestnut purée and the apple crisps, along with a few snipped chives.

Seafood chowder

This Irish take on a classic New England dish is perfect with a pint of Guinness. In the US they stick to clams in their chowder, but our mussels are too good to ignore and add a splash of striking colour.

Most mussels sold in the shops are now grown on ropes and come fairly free of both beards and barnacles. If you are picking your own off the foreshore, ask for local advice on the best place in order to ensure quality and safety. Barnacles tend to come by the bucket-load with these self-harvested specimens, but then you also get the added treat of free food. Mussels are traditionally not eaten during warmer 'without an "r" in the month' months, but farming and refrigeration have generally negated this rule

400g mussels, beards removed
250ml milk
250ml double cream
3 large waxy potatoes, peeled and cut into 1cm dice
2 onions, peeled and finely chopped
2 celery sticks, trimmed and finely chopped
100g bacon, finely diced
50g butter
1 tablespoon plain flour
pinch of cayenne pepper
200g firm white fish, such as monkfish, John Dory or sole, cut into bite-sized pieces
400g raw prawns

Wash the mussels thoroughly, discarding any that don't close on being handled or sharply tapped, and place in a large saucepan over a high heat with the lid on. Steam for 5-8 minutes or until the shellfish have just opened. If you cook them for too long they will shrink and dry up. Remove from the heat and, as soon as they are cool enough to handle, remove the empty half shell from each one and discard. Strain, reserving the liquid.

Heat the milk and cream together in another pan and poach the potato dice until just tender, about 8 minutes. Remove from the milk and cream mixture and set aside.

Cook the onions, celery and bacon in the butter for 10-15 minutes without colouring. Stir in the flour and cayenne pepper, and continue cooking for a further 2 minutes, stirring continuously. Pour in the strained liquid from the mussels along with the cream and milk and stir constantly to avoid lumps. Return the potatoes to the pan, add the white fish and prawns and poach for 5 minutes, or until everything is cooked. Return the mussels to the pan, heat through and check the seasoning before serving.

Sweetcorn chowder

This is a summer chowder, full of vibrancy and colour. Fresh corn on the cob is essential. In the recipe we suggest grilling the corn but you can also steam or boil it in the normal way.

1 red pepper
2 sweetcorn cobs
1 onion, finely chopped
50g butter
1 tablespoon flour
300ml milk
200ml vegetable stock
1 cinnamon stick (optional)
4 cloves
pinch of saffron stamens
1 tablespoon each roughly chopped basil, coriander and mint, to serve

Grill the red pepper until well blackened. Transfer to a bowl and cover with cling film. Leave for 10 minutes and uncover. As soon as it is cool enough to handle, core, remove the skin and seeds, and roughly chop. Cook the corn on a griddle plate until lightly charred. Scrape the kernels from the cobs using a sharp knife.

Gently sauté the onion in the butter for 10-15 minutes without allowing it to colour. Add the corn and continue cooking for a further 5 minutes. Add the flour, cook for 2 minutes without allowing to colour and pour in the milk and stock. Add the cinnamon stick, cloves and saffron, season with salt and pepper and continue cooking for a further 25-30 minutes.

Remove the cinnamon and cloves, and discard. Purée half the soup and combine with the unpuréed soup and the grilled peppers. Heat through
and check the seasoning. Serve with a generous sprinkling of the herbs.

Thai coconut and roast sweet potato soup

Thai soups are often rendered quite heavy by the overuse of coconut cream. The aim is to refresh and invigorate – all Thai food should be like this. A light hand with the coconut is to be encouraged.

2 sweet potatoes, peeled and cut into 3cm dice
4 tablespoons vegetable oil
1 onion, thinly sliced
2 leeks, trimmed and thinly sliced
4 thin slices of ginger
2 green chillies, or to taste, trimmed and thinly sliced
4 lemon grass stalks, tough exterior removed and soft interior thinly sliced and soaked in boiling water to soften
6 lime leaves, thinly sliced
2 tablespoons nam pla (fish sauce)
1 litre chicken stock
1 cup of thick coconut milk
Thai or purple basil to serve (green is fine if purple is unavailable)

Preheat the oven to 200°C/gas mark 6. Toss the sweet potato in 3 tablespoons of the vegetable oil, season well with salt and pepper and roast in the oven for 15-20 minutes, or until tender.

Add the remaining tablespoon of oil to a hot frying pan or wok and, just as it starts to smoke, add the onion and stir-fry for 3-4 minutes, or until well coloured. Add the leeks, ginger, chillies, lemon grass, lime leaves, fish sauce and the stock, and simmer for 10 minutes.

Add the sweet potato to the stock along with the coconut milk. Check the seasoning and serve with roughly torn basil. This soup can also be partially liquidised to give it a thicker consistency. The soup does not hold and therefore needs to be prepared and eaten right away.

Chicken ramen

This soup requires a good clear chicken stock, which means starting from scratch. Take two free-range chickens, remove the breasts and legs and place the carcasses in a saucepan, cover with cold water, bring to the boil, simmer for 3 minutes and then discard the water. This is to rid the dish of the impurities in the chicken. Rinse the carcasses under plenty of cold water and replace in the rinsed-out saucepan. Add a carrot, an onion, a celery stick, 1.5 litres of water, some salt and pepper and bring to the boil; lower the heat and simmer for 20 minutes. Strain and proceed. If you want to add even more body to the stock add 8 or 10 chicken wings.

serves 2

1 red chilli, or to taste, finely chopped, plus more, cut into thin slices, for garnish
1 garlic clove, finely chopped
3cm piece of ginger, peeled and grated
2 chicken breasts
600ml chicken stock
2 tablespoons fish sauce
250g fine thread egg noodles
2 handfuls of beansprouts
bunch of fresh coriander, leaves coarsely chopped and stems finely chopped
1 head of pak choi, shredded
1 red onion, halved and thinly sliced into fine half-moons
1 lime, quartered

Using the flat of a knife, mash the chilli, garlic and ginger together with a little salt. Spread over the chicken breasts and leave aside for half an hour.

Chargrill or sauté the chicken until cooked, about 8 minutes each side. Remove and allow to rest. Cut each breast at an angle into three slices. Bring the stock almost to the boil and add the fish sauce. Pour boiling water over the noodles and leave for 3 minutes, or until soft. Drain and refresh in cold water.

Mix the remaining ingredients, except the lime, together. Place the noodles in four preheated bowls and top with the vegetable mix. Pour over enough stock to cover, place three slices of chicken in each bowl and garnish with more chopped coriander, a lime quarter and maybe an extra chilli.

Variations on a ramen theme   The same basic recipe can be varied using a seared salmon darne, which is particularly delicious when marinated in teriyaki sauce.

Spiced tomato and kidney bean soup with avocado relish

1 onion
1 red pepper, cored and roughly chopped
olive oil
2 garlic cloves, peeled and crushed
quarter teaspoon each of ground cumin, ground coriander and sweet paprika
pinch of cayenne
half teaspoon dried oregano
1 x 400g tin of tomatoes
1 tablespoon tomato puree
half 400g tin of red kidney beans
300ml vegetable stock
juice of 1 lime
crème fraîche, to serve

for the avocado relish   1 avocado, stoned, peeled and roughly chopped   juice of 1 lime or lemon
half teaspoon finely chopped red chilli or to taste   1 tablespoon finely diced red onion
pinch each of ground cumin and ground coriander   1 tablespoon chopped fresh coriander
4 tablespoons of olive oil

for the Parmesan toasts   4 slices of French bread   1 garlic clove, halved
2 tablespoons grated Parmesan

Gently sauté the onion and red pepper in 2 tablespoons olive oil for 10-15 minutes, or until soft and lightly coloured. Add the garlic, spices and herbs and salt and pepper to taste. Cook for a further 2 minutes and then add the tomatoes and the purée, drained kidney beans and stock and simmer for 20 minutes. Check that the pepper and onion are soft, then allow to cool for 5 minutes and liquidise. Stir in lime juice to taste and gently reheat, checking the seasoning.

To make the relish, combine all the ingredients except the oil and season, then stir in the olive oil.

To make the Parmesan toasts, brush the slices of bread with a little olive oil, rub with the cut side of the garlic clove and grill on one side until golden brown. Turn over and sprinkle over the Parmesan, then put back under the grill briefly.

Serve the soup in warmed bowls, each with a dollop of crème fraîche, a generous drizzle of the relish and a Parmesan toast.

Chickpea soup with goat's cheese and gremolata

4 garlic cloves, smashed and roughly chopped (don't worry about the skin)

4 tablespoons extra virgin olive oil

1 teaspoon finely chopped rosemary

1 x 400g tin of chopped tomatoes

2 x 400g tins of chickpeas rinsed and drained

300ml chicken stock

100g goat's cheese, crumbled, to serve

for the gremolata

zest of 1 lemon   1 garlic clove, very finely chopped   2 tablespoons finely chopped flat-leaf parsley

Sauté the garlic in 4 tablespoons of olive oil over a moderate heat until golden brown. Remove the garlic and discard. This flavoured oil gives the soup a subtle garlic flavour; if the garlic were to stay in, it would burn. Add the rosemary, chopped tomatoes and chickpeas, and sauté gently for 15-20 minutes, or until the oil separates. Add the chicken stock, season with salt and pepper and simmer for 15 minutes.

For the gremolata, combine the lemon zest, chopped garlic and parsley. To serve, crumble the goat's cheese over the soup and sprinkle over the gremolata.

Ham hock and split pea soup with mint relish

This is a delicious, robust, full flavoured dish with quite a lot of zing from the relish. If you want to enrich it further, consider grating over some Parmesan to serve.

2 ham hocks
bunch of parsley
2 carrots
2 celery sticks
500g split peas, soaked overnight and rinsed in several changes of water
2 onions, peeled

for the mint relish
juice of 1 lemon
1 teaspoon black mustard seeds
2 tablespoons chopped mint
half red onion, finely chopped
2 tomatoes, deseeded, cored and diced
olive oil

Combine the ham hocks, parsley, carrots, celery, split peas and onions in a large pot. Slowly bring to the boil and simmer gently for $2^{1}/_{2}$ to 3 hours, skimming off any scum that rises to the surface.

Remove the parsley, carrots, celery and onion and discard. Remove the ham hocks, ease the meat away from the bone, discarding the bone and surplus fat, and return the meat to the soup. Liquidise briefly.

Combine all the ingredients for the relish except the oil, then drizzle in enough olive oil to form a thick paste and serve as a dollop in the soup.

For the photograph, we liquidised the soup without the meat, shredding it into a neat pile. This makes for a slightly more elegant way of serving.

STARTERS

First impressions will dictate how your guests feel about their whole evening. Starters are there to impress, excite and introduce. However, this does not mean they need to be complicated, time-consuming, or involve a lot of shopping.

A few slices of Parma ham and salami, a slice of good pâté, even an interesting mixed salad is enticing enough when made with first-class ingredients providing lots of colour. These are the kinds of dishes that can be prepared in moments, rather than slaved over for hours before your guests arrive.

Keep it simple and go for colour. The freshest salad leaves, organic eggs with deep yellow yolks and firm whites, olives that glisten with rich, meaty flesh. Specialist shops rather than supermarkets are worth seeking out.

Don't forget the more obvious ingredients; a good chicken liver pâté spread on toast with some well dressed salad leaves, Parma ham with a few well-chosen char-grilled vegetables, or hot-smoked and flaky smoked salmon or tuna with a dill-rich dressing on thinly sliced brown bread. Celebrate the seasons. What looks and eats well does not have to cost the earth.

Bread may seem like a basic food, but there is a world of difference between a good and a bad loaf. Flour, yeast, salt, water and time are the only ingredients – along with the soul of the baker. Relax and indulge in one of the most ancient of foods

WHITE YEAST BREAD €2.60

Crostini and bruschetta

Crostini and bruschetta may sound elaborate, but both can really translate as 'things on toast'. The essential difference between the two is that with crostini the oil is put on before the bread is toasted, with bruschetta it goes on afterwards, often with a generous rub of garlic. You would generally avoid putting an oily topping on crostini, so a tomato, olive, olive oil and basil topping; for example, would be more likely on bruschetta than crostini. The possibilities for toppings are endless, but don't be tempted to include too much in any one topping, you need to taste all the ingredients, including the bread. Sliced white is out, good country-style bread is in. Sourdough makes particularly good bruschetta, if you can get hold of it.

Neither bruschetta nor crostini can be totally prepared in advance, they go chewy. You can toast crostini in advance, and then put on the topping just before you serve. Bruschetta do need to be done at the last moment; the heat from the bread is essential to the whole experience.

Bruschetta
Toast or grill – you can use the barbecue or griddle pan – slices of good-quality country bread on both sides, rub with garlic, drizzle with oil and finish with your chosen topping. In Italy bruschetta are often eaten like this, with just the olive oil to flavour, which can be fantastic if you have really good extra virgin olive oil. There is no need to peel the garlic you are rubbing on to the bread, simply cut a clove in half and rub the cut side on to the bread. If you are doing larger quantities, cut a whole head in half horizontally through the cloves. Again there is no need to peel off the skin.

Crostini
Slice a French stick, ciabatta, or other good quality bread, lay the slices on a wire rack or a roasting tray. Drizzle sparingly with olive oil and toast in an oven preheated to 220°C/gas mark 7 for a scant 4-5 minutes. (Keep an eye on them, they burn remarkably easily towards the end of the cooking.) Remove, allow to cool and stack upright until used. Like toast, if you stack them too closely as they cool they will go soggy.

The toppings below provide enough for 6-8 people as a starter assuming you are going to pick three to four different ones.

Green or black olive paste
200g pitted green or black olives   2 dessertspoons capers, well rinsed
2 garlic cloves, finely chopped and mashed with a little salt   2 tablespoons finely chopped parsley
4 anchovy fillets, well rinsed   juice and zest of 1 lemon   about 200ml good-quality extra virgin olive oil

Finely chop all the solid ingredients, mix together and whisk in enough olive oil to form a paste. Season with salt, pepper and lemon juice and serve. This will keep, covered with a little extra olive oil, in the fridge for a few days.

Grilled vegetables   2 red peppers   1 aubergine   2 courgettes   olive oil   1 dessertspoon thyme
1 tablespoon finely chopped parsley   3 garlic cloves

Grill the peppers until well charred, remove and place in a bowl. Cover with cling film and allow them to steam for at least 10 minutes. Remove the film and, when cool enough to handle, remove the skin and seeds. If you are in hurry, you can do this under cold running water.

Slice the aubergine and courgettes thinly, rub sparingly with olive oil and grill – preferably on a ridged griddle pan, but a conventional grill is fine – until lightly charred on both sides. Add to the bowl with the peppers. You will probably have to do the grilling in batches, so season with salt, pepper and the herbs as you go.

Smash the garlic and add to the bowl of hot vegetables along with the thyme. Set aside for 30 minutes to infuse. Discard the garlic as you pile the vegetables on to your bruschetta.

Spinach, feta and sun-dried tomatoes   1 tablespoon finely chopped shallots   2 tablespoons olive oil
2 garlic cloves, thinly sliced   450g spinach   2 tablespoons roughly chopped semi-sun-dried tomatoes
1 red chilli, trimmed and finely chopped   75g feta, crumbled

Soften the shallots in the oil for 5 minutes without allowing to colour. Add the garlic and a minute later the spinach, turning to coat in the oil and allow to wilt without it catching. Stir in the tomatoes and chilli, remove from the heat and allow to cool. Gently squeeze out the excess moisture and roughly chop. Stir in the feta and serve.

Buffalo mozzarella, plum tomato and rocket pesto   1 good-quality buffalo mozzarella
2 tomatoes, quartered, cored and deseeded   bunch of rocket, stems removed   1 dessertspoon pine nuts
1 garlic clove, finely chopped   1 dessertspoon grated Parmesan   about 6 tablespoons olive oil
2 handfuls of baby salad leaves to serve

Slice the mozzarella and combine with the tomatoes. Combine the rocket, pine nuts and garlic in a pestle and mortar with a seasoning of salt and pepper and mash to a pulp. Add the cheese and, stirring, work in enough olive oil to form a loose paste.

Mix the mozzarella and tomatoes with the baby salad leaves and pile on to bruschetta. Spoon over the rocket pesto and serve.The flavour of pine nuts can be enhanced by gently sautéing them in butter, or toasting in a dry frying pan with a little salt. This treatment is also useful with whole spices, to bring out and round off their initially harsh flavours.

Grilled vegetables

Fried eggs and prosciutto   2 tablespoons olive oil   12 quail's eggs   100g Parma or Serrano ham
a little truffle oil (optional)

Heat the oil in a frying pan over a moderate heat and fry the quail's eggs until just set. Gently tear the prosciutto into pieces, place on top of your crostini or bruschetta and finish off with an egg or two. Season with
salt and pepper. You can also drizzle over a little truffle oil for an added flourish.

Braised red peppers, goat's cheese croûte and black olives

This is a simple rustic Spanish dish, a favourite of Leylie's. It's a perfect dish which doesn't have to have a kitchen sink of extras added. Make it good and simple. It actually improves if made the day before as the flavours have time to amalgamate.

1 onion, finely chopped

3 tablespoons olive oil, plus more to serve

4 garlic cloves, finely chopped

1 x 400g tin of tomatoes

glass of red wine

1 dessertspoon picked thyme

1 dessertspoon picked oregano

pinch of sugar

4 red peppers

2 yellow peppers

4 slices goat's cheese

8 black olives

8 sun-dried tomatoes

Gently sauté the onion in the olive oil over a moderate heat for 10 minutes without colouring. Add the garlic, stir to coat in the oil and then add the tomatoes, red wine, herbs and sugar. Season with salt and pepper and reduce by half over a low heat to concentrate the flavours, about 15 minutes.

Roast the peppers under a hot grill, turning so they blacken all over. Transfer to a bowl, cover with cling film and peel and deseed as soon as they are cool enough to handle. Tear each into 6 strips, but don't be too exact, the finished dish looks better if they are mismatched. Add to the tomato mixture, along with any juices, and gently reheat.

Transfer into individual terracotta or heat-proof bowls, lay a slice of goat's cheese in the middle and flash under the grill. Garnish with the black olives and sun-dried tomatoes and a good slick of olive oil. Serve with lots of crusty bread to mop up.

Braised globe artichokes with mint and lemon

8 artichokes
2 lemons
1 tablespoon finely chopped shallot
2 carrots, finely chopped
1 celery stick, finely chopped
4 tablespoons olive oil
2 glasses of white wine
large bunch of mint, finely chopped

Cut the top third from each artichoke. Rub with the cut side of one of the lemons as you go to stop discolouration. Then trim the stem and remove the outside bottom three layers of leaves, or until the leaves inside become soft and pliable.

Gently soften the shallot, carrot and celery in the olive oil for 10 minutes without allowing them to colour. Add the artichokes and toss in the oil, then add the wine, season with salt and cover with foil or a lid. Braise over a gentle heat for 30-40 minutes or until the artichokes are cooked. Boil off the liquid for the last 10 minutes by removing the lid. Allow to cool to room temperature, toss with the mint, check the seasoning and serve.

Eimer's baked red peppers with tomatoes, mozzarella and anchovies

2 red peppers
4-5 tablespoons olive oil, plus more to serve
2 garlic cloves, thinly sliced
2 tomatoes
1 mozzarella
8 anchovy fillets

Preheat the oven to 180°C/gas mark 4. Halve the peppers, scoop out the seeds and lay, cut side up, on a roasting tray. Pour over the olive oil. Scatter over the garlic and bake in the preheated oven for 40 minutes, or until slightly wilted. Plunge the tomatoes into boiling water for 30 seconds, remove and skin, halve, scoop out the seeds and place inside the pepper halves. Cut the mozzarella into chunks and put inside the tomatoes. Return to the oven for 5 minutes so the mozzarella just melts. Criss-cross the anchovies on top and serve with bread and extra olive oil if required. This is an ideal dinner party starter as it can be prepared in advance.

Melissa's roast figs, garlic cream cheese and Parma ham

This simple yet surprisingly delicious starter is borrowed from Melissa Webb, a professional cook with oodles of flair. Watch out for fresh figs towards the end of the summer.

2 garlic cloves, peeled and finely chopped and crushed with a little salt
4 tablespoons cream cheese
8 figs, halved
8 slices of Parma ham
2 heads of chicory, shredded
2 tablespoons olive oil
1 teaspoon white wine vinegar

Preheat the oven to 200°C/gas mark 6. Mix the garlic into the cream cheese and season with salt and pepper. Place a teaspoon of this mixture on each fig half and wrap with half a slice of Parma ham. Roast in the pre-heated oven for 5 minutes.

Toss the chicory with the olive oil and white wine vinegar, and season with salt and pepper.

Serve the figs with a neat pile of the dressed chicory.

Fennel salad

2 fennel bulbs, trimmed and quartered
1 tablespoon sherry vinegar
4 tablespoons olive oil
juice of 1 lemon
100g Parmesan, shaved

Trim the fennel bulbs and slice them as thinly as possible vertically. Blanch the slices briefly in boiling salted water (one minute is sufficient).

Drain and put in a bowl with the sherry vinegar, olive oil and the lemon juice. Season well with pepper and a little salt and toss. Cover with cling film and leave for an hour. Divide between 4 plates, scatter over the Parmesan and serve.

Panzanella

Chefs often talk about peasant Italian food, well this is about as peasant as Italian food comes – a salad which uses up stale bread by dressing it with a few inexpensive ingredients, probably originally not much more than tomatoes and olive oil. Remarkably refreshing on a hot day, this is a very basic version, more elaborate recipes toast the bread, but this seems to us to rather miss the point.

2 red peppers
1 stale loaf of ciabatta bread, cut into bite-sized chunks
500g tomatoes, cored, deseeded and roughly chopped
2 garlic cloves, crushed to a paste with a little salt
olive oil
2 tablespoons red wine vinegar
1 tablespoon capers, well rinsed
100g black olives, pitted
8 anchovy fillets
bunch of basil

Grill the peppers until charred all over, put in a bowl and cover with cling film for 10 minutes. Remove the cling film and, as soon as they are cool enough to handle, peel, core and deseed. Tear into strips and place in a bowl along with the chunks of bread, tomatoes, garlic, a generous slug of olive oil, the vinegar, capers and olives. Toss so everything is well coated. Pile on to 4 plates, scatter over the anchovies and basil and serve.

Char-grilled peppers, capers and Parmesan

4 red peppers (or 2 red and 2 yellow)
1 tablespoon well-rinsed capers
4 tablespoons olive oil
1 tablespoon balsamic vinegar
1 tablespoon shaved Parmesan

Grill the peppers until black, place in a bowl, cover with cling film and allow to steam for 10 minutes. Remove the cling film and, when cool enough to handle, peel and deseed. Cut into thin strips and combine in a shallow bowl with the strained juices from the peppers, the capers, olive oil, balsamic and a seasoning of salt and pepper. Scatter over the Parmesan and serve.

Red and yellow peppers are ripe, green are unripe and not nearly as easily digested. There is a huge variation in the quality of peppers, some come with a deep, rich colouring, others are almost translucent. These latter tend to collapse in the cooking, their water content is too predominant. The flesh of a good pepper is actually quite meaty, both in flavour and texture

Cannellini, kidney and French bean salad with grain mustard dressing

Beans have distinctive flavours and textures, often only really shown when they are combined together.

12 slices of streaky bacon, cut into lardons

450g French beans, trimmed

4 tablespoons extra virgin olive oil

1 garlic clove, finely chopped

1 teaspoon white wine vinegar

1 x 400g tin of cannellini beans, drained and well rinsed

1 x 400g tin of kidney beans, drained and well rinsed

1 teaspoon grainy mustard

2 tablespoons finely chopped flat leaf parsley

1 tablespoon roughly chopped chervil

1 dessertspoon finely chopped chives

8 cherry tomatoes, halved

1 teaspoon finely chopped fresh red chilli

Sauté the bacon until golden and crispy and drain on kitchen paper.

Cook the French beans in boiling salted water for 4 minutes, or until just cooked but still al dente. Drain and toss in the oil, garlic and vinegar while still warm.

Combine with the bacon, the remaining ingredients and a seasoning of salt and pepper. Toss everything so it is well coated and distribute on 4 plates.

Falafel, pickles and pitta

200g dried chickpeas or dried broad beans. soaked overnight
4 garlic cloves, finely chopped
1 onion, finely chopped
bunch of coriander, roughly chopped
1 teaspoon ground cumin
1 red chilli, finely chopped
vegetable oil, for frying

Rinse the chickpeas in plenty of fresh water, drain and transfer to a food processor or blender along with the remaining ingredients and blend to a rough paste. You may need to add a little water. Refrigerate for an hour.

Dip your hands in water and mould the paste into squashed ping-pong-ball-sized spheres. Heat 6 tablespoons of oil and, when hot, shallow-fry the falafel until golden. Turn over and cook the other sides. Transfer to kitchen paper and allow to drain. Serve warm with a selection of pickles (bought from good ethnic stores and delicatessens), warmed pitta bread and the tzatziki on page 45.

Mezze plate

Mezze is a Middle Eastern idea, a selection of tasty morsels similar to Spanish tapas. Both are an opportunity to enjoy an assortment of tastes and textures and both work as convivial starters as sharing is encouraged. Accompany with a glass of cold white wine or sherry.

Spiced lamb koftas

Make up half the recipe quantity of the Spiced lamb burger (page 188). Form the mixture into small balls, sprinkle with sesame seeds and cook for 20 minutes in an oven preheated to 180°C/gas mark 4, turning them halfway through cooking so they brown evenly. Drizzle over a few extra sesame seeds and a teaspoon of sesame oil before serving.

Tzatziki

1 cucumber   450g Greek-style yoghurt   bunch of fresh mint, finely chopped
1 garlic clove, finely chopped and mashed with a little salt

Grate the cucumber into a sieve and toss with a teaspoon of salt. Set aside over a bowl for 10 minutes. Rinse well and squeeze out as much liquid as possible. Combine with all the other ingredients and set aside for 20 minutes. Stir, check seasoning and serve.

Hummus

This delicious Middle Eastern starter works as well with crudités as toasted pitta bread and is also delicious when added to sandwiches.

125g chickpeas, soaked overnight   2 garlic cloves, finely chopped and mashed to a pulp   juice of 2 lemons
2 tablespoons tahini   olive oil, to dress   pinch of hot paprika

Rinse the chickpeas and simmer in fresh water for an hour or until tender. Drain, reserving the cooking water. Blitz the chickpeas in a food processor or liquidiser along with the garlic, lemon juice, tahini and seasoning to taste. Add enough of the cooking liquid to give a consistency similar to that of thick cream. Spoon into a bowl and refrigerate.

To serve, drizzle over a generous quantity of olive oil and dust with the paprika.

Clockwise: spiced lamb koftas, tzatziki and hummus

Pulses

From nutty chickpeas to sweet and meaty lentils, from creamy butter beans to smooth and silky split red lentils, the world of pulses has much to offer the cook. Some say pulses take time, but that is only in the planning. A little foresight and your overnight soaking is taken care of. If you are really in a hurry, good tinned pulses are a useful shortcut and make sense if numbers are reasonable. In the cafés, it is not really practical, but two tins of chickpeas will give you hummus for eight which has more zing, character and depth of flavour than anything you will buy in a shop. In general, all pulses thrive on being dressed whilst warm and benefit from good robust flavours: olive oil, garlic, lemon juice, ground cumin and coriander. Herbs provide body and character, but should be added as the pulses cool or they lose their colour. Below are a selection of the pulses we use most frequently.

Lentils   There are various types, but the Puy version, shown in the picture, are considered some of the best. In Italy the first lentils of the season are often offered as a course on their own, braised gently with vegetables and herbs to show off their sweet, meaty flavour.

Black beans   Used in rich, meaty stews in South America and in black bean soup, the latter laced with cumin, coriander and chilli. This sweet but robust bean packs a fair punch and is best partnered with other strong flavours.

Split peas   The ideal partner for a ham bone or knuckle of bacon, these dusty green pulses are perfect in soups and casseroles, providing a wintry, homely flavour that picks up other ingredients well.

Split red lentils   Easily cooked, these are one of the sweetest pulses and are inclined to collapse easily, so take care when cooking if a purée is not the desired end result. Split red lentils take the same time to cook as basmati rice and together they make a colourful and well-flavoured pilaf.

Kidney beans   Excellent not only in chilli con carne, but also in beef stews and curries generally, as well as salads. Kidney beans keep their shape well but are resistant to picking up other flavours, so make sure to dress while still warm and use strong robust ingredients like garlic and mustard.

Butter beans   Perfect for salads, these sweetish, butter-textured beans absorb flavours, particularly dressings, very well and are excellent in salads. Take care not to overcook them or the skins are inclined to flake off.

Chickpeas   Golden nutty nuggets and by far one of our most popular pulses. They need a good overnight soaking and cooking – nobody likes al dente chickpeas. After that they are useful in stews and casseroles with a Spanish or North African slant as well as the continually popular hummus.

Clockwise: chicpeas, butter beans, black beans, split red lentils, kidney beans, split peas, Puy lentils

Roast tomato and mozzarella galette with basil

1 sheet (about 200g) of puff pastry

4 teaspoons tapenade or black olive paste (see page 33)

6 slow-roasted tomatoes, or (in the summer) slices of ripe tomatoes (see page 92)

2 buffalo mozzarella

2 handfuls of basil

12 semi-sun-dried tomatoes, roughly chopped

Preheat the oven to 200°C/gas mark 6 and line a shallow baking tray with baking paper. Roll out the pastry and cut out 4 discs using a 10cm pastry cutter. Prick well with a fork and place on the prepared baking tray. Cover with more baking parchment and weigh down with a second shallow baking tray. Bake in the preheated oven for 10-15 minutes. The two baking trays keep the pastry rounds in a circular shape, otherwise they tend to become ovals.

Spread the tapenade on each pastry disc. Arrange the slow-roasted tomatoes on top and then the mozzarella. Return to the oven for a few minutes, or until the cheese starts to melt.

Scatter the basil and semi-sun-dried tomatoes decoratively on top.

Duck terrine

makes one 1kg terrine

225g each of dried apricots and dried prunes, roughly chopped

about 8 tablespoons brandy

600g duck livers, cleaned and trimmed

600g butter

2 garlic cloves, crushed

1 tablespoon thyme leaves

225g duck confit, shredded (see page 204)

110g roasted pistachios

4 bay leaves

50g dried cranberries or zeresk berries

clarified butter, to seal

Put the apricots and prunes to soak in three tablespoons of brandy overnight. Line a 1kg loaf tin with cling film. Cook the livers on a low heat in 100g of the butter. Add 4 tablespoons of brandy and remove from the heat. Blitz in a food processor. Deglaze the pan with the remaining tablespoon of brandy, add the garlic and thyme and scrape into the food processor and blend, adding the remaining butter. Make sure the livers are not too hot or the butter will separate.

Transfer the puréed liver mixture to a bowl and add the confit and pistachios. Season to taste. Transfer to the lined tin, cover with the bay leaves, the dried cranberries and a thin layer of clarified butter. Allow to cool and solidify. When slicing, rinse the knife in hot water each time and wipe clean. Serve with the kumquats below.

Pickled kumquats with orange slices   *makes about 2kg*   900g kumquats, halved lengthwise
and pips removed   8 large oranges, halved and thinly sliced   1.1kg sugar   1 litre white wine vinegar
3 large cinnamon sticks   32 whole cloves

Put the kumquats and orange slices in a saucepan and cover with water. Bring to the boil and simmer until the orange slices are tender, about 20 minutes. In a separate saucepan, dissolve the sugar in the white wine vinegar. Add the cinnamon and cloves, and stir until it comes to the boil.

Drain the liquid off the oranges and reserve. Place the kumquats and orange slices in the vinegar mixture and cook for a further 15 minutes, or until translucent and slightly candied. You may need to add some of the reserved orange liquid to cover. Transfer to a large sterilized airtight container, seal and leave to mature for three to four weeks.

To clarify butter, gently heat in a small saucepan. Pour off the clear butter, leaving the milky solids behind.

Scallops, pea purée and mint vinaigrette

1 dessertspoon finely chopped shallots

1 dessertspoon butter

2 tablespoons white wine

200g frozen peas, or better still, petit pois

2 tablespoons double cream

2 lemons

1 tablespoon white wine vinegar

4 tablespoons of olive oil, plus a little more for coating the scallops

bunch of mint, finely chopped

8 large scallops

juice of 1 lemon, plus lemon quarters to serve

Gently soften the shallots in the butter for 5 minutes, add the wine and boil it away without allowing the shallots to colour. Add the peas and cream, and cook for barely 1 minute. Purée or push through a mouli-légume. Season with salt, pepper and lemon juice.

Combine the white wine vinegar, olive oil and mint, and season with salt and pepper.

Preheat a frying pan or griddle pan until really hot. Gently toss the scallops in a little olive oil and then season with salt. Place on the hot surface of the pan and leave them alone. Cook for 2 minutes, turn and cook for 2 minutes on the other side.

Gently reheat the pea purée and spoon on to 4 warmed plates. Place the scallops on top and spoon over some of the mint vinaigrette. Serve with a lemon quarter.

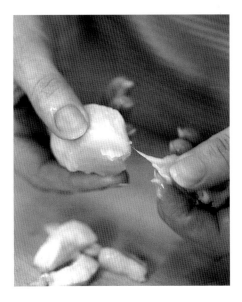

We don't cook the scallop coral with the scallop as it over-cooks and goes hard by the time the scallop is done. Removing it is not difficult (you can cook it separately) and at the same time you need to remove the slightly gristly bit which is where the scallop is attached to its shell.

Prawns pil-pil

You must use uncooked shelled prawns, available at good fish counters and fishmongers. Cooked prawns are not suitable for this dish, they simply dry up and taste like cardboard.

800g uncooked shelled prawns (see above)
300ml extra virgin olive oil
6 garlic cloves, coarsely chopped
1 teaspoon dried chilli flakes, or to taste, or finely chopped fresh red chilli
1 tablespoon finely chopped parsley
2 lemons, to serve

Remove the shells from the prawns if necessary. Heat the oil over a medium heat and, when almost smoking, add the prawns. Toss in the hot oil for 2 minutes. Add the garlic and chilli and continue cooking in the hot oil for a scant 2 minutes, or until the prawns are cooked. Take care not to burn the garlic.

Just before serving, add the parsley, season with salt and pepper and accompany with lemon halves and lots of crusty bread to mop up the infused oil. The best thing to drink with this is chilled dry sherry, a perfect match.

This dish works particularly well when cooked in individual terracotta bowls, when they can be brought – bubbling – straight to the table.

Variations   Add coriander, lime juice and chilli sauce at the end and serve with chilled beer in place of the sherry. As a vegetarian alternative you can do the same dish with button onions and mushrooms.

Langoustines are one of the ocean's real treats – sweet, meaty and succulent. Feasts do not get better than this. Set your knife and fork aside. Fingers are the only way.

Potato pancake, smoked salmon, créme fraîche and caviar

These pancakes are quite delicate and do burn easily. The main difficulty is the potatoes, which come in a huge variety of types, some floury, some waxy and there is much variety throughout the year – what may be good in May, will be watery and hopeless in December. At the cafés, we tend to use the Irish variety roosters all year round for their consistency and because we are generally looking for a floury potato. If the pancakes do look as if they might burn, only colour them lightly on each side and then finish cooking in a hot oven.

serves 6

300g floury potatoes

3 eggs, plus the whites of 2 more eggs

2 heaped tablespoons self-raising flour

75ml full-fat milk

75ml double cream

oil, for frying

200g smoked salmon, thinly sliced

150ml crème fraîche

small pot of caviar or lumpfish roe to serve

1 tablespoon finely chopped chives, plus some more to garnish

Preheat the oven to 200°C/gas mark 6. Peel the potatoes, roughly chop them and boil until tender. Dry in kitchen paper and mash or work through a mouli-légume or sieve.

Beat the 3 whole eggs and the flour into the mashed potatoes. Combine the milk and cream, bring to the boil, remove from the heat and whisk into the potato mixture.

Whisk the egg whites until stiff and gently fold into the batter. Place baking rings or a scone cutter in a frying pan and pour in a generous quantity of oil. When hot, ladle in the mixture and cook over a medium heat until just brown. Remove the ring and turn over using a spatula. Finish cooking on top of the stove or transfer to the preheated oven for 5 minutes to cook through.

To serve gently pile smoked salmon on top of each pancake. Top with crème fraîche and a neat dollop of caviar. Season with salt and pepper and place a small pile of chives to one side.

BRUNCH

The sun is shining, you've enjoyed a lie-in and the day holds little or no structure beyond having friends round and enjoying yourselves. Brunch is informal, a meal to fit the mood, day and circumstances.

For some, this includes soothing cereal and yoghurt, perhaps topped with fresh fruit. For others it's bacon sandwiches and lots of black coffee. Eggs seem to feature in most people's wish lists, but again there are no rules; omelettes, frittatas or tortillas are all delicious. What does matter are the eggs - go for those from small producers who look after their hens.

Yoghurt blitzed with summer berries, mangos or strawberries will ease you into the day, while a bloody Mary will fire you up and cure any lasting hangover. Pancakes are a breeze, whether paired with bacon and maple syrup, smoked salmon or more fresh fruit and yoghurt.

Be generous with quantities, having got up late, read the papers, and missed breakfast most guests are anticipating lunch and keen to graze for hours. After all, it's not every day of the week you can afford to be quite so relaxed.

Smoothies

Some insist on yoghurt, others are indifferent. The fruit may be sweetened or unsweetened. For some the occasion is breakfast, for others it's a late-afternoon pick-me-up. Whatever the time of day, smoothies are endlessly variable and always rewarding. All that health delivered in delicious glassfuls of goodness.

The fruit used varies depending on the season and it is hard to be precise concerning quantities. A strawberry in July needs little help, in April it is crying out for honey or some other sweetener. Half the fun of smoothies is playing around with ingredients and this goes for the sweetness element too. Taste often and adjust accordingly. The one word of warning is to be restrained – too many ingredients and things all start to get confusing.

The following are a few specific suggestions but they are there only as a starting point. Time to let your creativity loose. Bananas figure in most recipes as they help to give the smoothie body. We use organic fruit juice in the cafés as this provides a deeper, more satisfying flavour. Each recipe should provide 4 good-sized glasses. Make and serve, smoothies are not known for their keeping qualities.

Passion fruit and pineapple   1 mango   6 passion fruit   1 small small fresh pineapple   1 banana
2 cups chilled orange juice

Put all the ingredients in a food processor and blend until smooth. The smoothie is best enjoyed immediately after processing, so to get it nice and cold you can chill (or even freeze) the fruit or add some ice cubes to the mix.

Mango madness   4 mangos   2 bananas   2 cups of apple or orange juice

Summer berries
2 cups of frozen mixed berries   2 bananas
2 cups of apple or orange juice or Greek-style yoghurt

Strawberry and orange
4 cups of strawberries   2 bananas
2 cups of orange juice

Grapefruit, Campari and mint
juice of 3 grapefruit   1 glass of Campari
1 tablespoon finely chopped mint
2 bananas

From the top: Passion fruit and pineapple, summer berries, strawberry and orange

Granola

Popular in America, this is essentially a cooked muesli, a combination of healthy ingredients combined and roasted to a golden crunchiness. Serve with yoghurt, honey and fruit compote for a real sunshine brunch.

75g dark brown sugar
1 tablespoon honey
100g rolled oats
225g oat flakes
100g wheat flakes
100g barley flakes
50g rye flakes
25g toasted pumpkin seeds
25g linseeds
100ml sunflower oil

40g millet flakes/wheatgerm
150g sultanas
50g chopped dates
50g chopped figs
50g dried banana
80g toasted hazelnuts
25g pine nuts
25g slivered almonds

Preheat the oven to 170°C/gas mark 3. Combine the first 9 ingredients along with the oil, spread out in a roasting tray and bake in the preheated oven for 30-40 minutes, or until golden brown. You need to stir the mixture around every 10 minutes to prevent uneven browning. Allow to cool.

Combine with the millet flakes, fruit and nuts. Stored in an airtight tin, this will keep for several weeks.

Most of these ingredients are available in health food shops. Sold in 100g or 500g packs, there is undoubtedly a need to store the excess. You can multiply the above and pack the excess in kilner jars – they make ideal presents.

Omelettes, tortillas and frittatas

The quality of eggs you buy varies hugely, depending on many factors like the breed, diet and husbandry of the hens producing the eggs. Make sure your eggs are free-range at least, organic is even better. Look for deep yellow yolks and a white that is thick and viscous. Small suppliers are generally better than larger

In the cafés, we tend more towards frittata than omelette, although some would say tortilla. While there may be a world of difference between a light, fluffy French-style omelette that needs to be eaten immediately and a frittata, both the latter and a tortilla are much the same – slowly cooked eggs that set into a 'cake' and will keep for several hours. Good lunchtime food, they can also be sliced and made into a delicious sandwich.

To say that anything can go in an omelette is a little unhelpful. Anything can, almost, but you need to think things through. As a rule, stick to no more than three main ingredients, otherwise one ingredient starts to cancel another out. And try to keep to a theme; spinach and blue cheese have their origins as partners in French cuisine, so bacon is fine, but this is no time for coriander.

Fish and meat need to be cooked before being added, while saladings and herbs – rocket, spinach, sage – will be cooked by the hot eggs. Each of the following frittatas is based on using a 28cm frying pan and will serve 6-8 people. A good frying pan is essential, something nonstick and weighty.

Mushroom and thyme omelette *serves 2*

125g button mushrooms, thinly sliced   2 tablespoons finely chopped shallots   2 tablespoons butter, plus a little for cooking the eggs   1 dessertspoon picked thyme   freshly grated nutmeg   2 tablespoons double cream 1 tablespoon finely chopped parsley   6 eggs, lightly beaten and seasoned

Gently sauté the mushrooms and shallots in the butter for 10 minutes. Add the thyme and season with nutmeg, salt and pepper. Stir in the cream and parsley and set aside.

In a clean frying pan, melt the remaining butter and pour in the eggs. With a wooden spoon, draw the edges in to let more of the liquid flow into contact with the heat. As the eggs start to set properly on the bottom, pour in the mushroom mixture. Finish cooking, fold over and serve.

Gubbeen bacon, spinach and potato frittata

250g smoked Gubbeen streaky bacon, cut into lardons   2 potatoes, cubed   3 tablespoons vegetable oil   4 handfuls of baby spinach   15 large eggs, lightly beaten and well seasoned

Sauté the lardons in a dry frying pan over a moderate heat until crispy. Heat the oil, add the potato and shallow fry for 10 minutes, or until cooked. Add the eggs, bacon and spinach and stir gently until the bottom starts to set. Cook for 5 to 10 minutes and finish off in the oven, or under a moderate grill.

Potato and sage frittata
4 potatoes, peeled and thinly sliced
1 onion, halved and cut into thin half-moon slices   6 tablespoons olive oil   handful of picked sage leaves
15 large eggs, lightly beaten and seasoned

Sauté the potatoes and onion in 4 tablespoons of olive oil until cooked, about 10-15 minutes. Add the sage leaves and continue cooking for 2 minutes. Pour in the eggs. Cook for 5 to 10 minutes and finish off in the oven, or under a moderate grill.

Cherry tomato, chive and basil frittata
2 garlic cloves, unpeeled   4 tablespoons olive oil
1 punnet slow-roasted cherry tomatoes, (see page 111)   15 eggs, lightly beaten and seasoned   2 tablespoons grated Parmesan   2 generous handfuls of basil   2 tablespoons finely chopped chives

Smash the garlic cloves and poach in the olive oil for 5 minutes or until golden-brown. Discard the garlic. Add the tomatoes and cook for 15 minutes, or until the mixture starts to thicken. Allow to cool and then stir into the eggs, along with the Parmesan, basil and chives and some salt and pepper.

Lightly oil the pan, pour in the egg mixture and cook until set, finishing the top off under a preheated grill.

Pea, mint and French bean frittata
200g French beans   100g peas
15 eggs, lightly beaten and seasoned   2 tablespoons freshly grated Parmesan   2 tablespoons finely chopped mint
1 tablespoon butter

Blanch the beans and peas separately in boiling salted water until cooked, drain and refresh in cold water (this helps to keep their colour). Combine with the eggs, Parmesan, mint and some seasoning.

Melt the butter in a frying pan, pour in the egg mixture and cook until set, finishing the top off under a pre-heated grill.

Other ideas
Smoked salmon, dill and cream cheese   Rocket, goat's cheese and semi-sun-dried tomatoes   Roast Mediterranean vegetables and goat's cheese   Chorizo, red peppers and coriander.

For quantities, be guided by the size of your pan and bear in mind the egg element is also important, it is not just there to bind everything together, it should also add flavour.

Gubbeen bacon, spinach and potato frittata page 65

Crispy bacon and maple syrup on buttermilk pancakes

Pancakes

From wafer-thin, to decidedly thick, made using water, or with rich and comforting buttermilk, pancakes are perfect comfort food. The question of thick or thin is a matter of taste, we tend to make thinner ones in the café, but then we are usually stuffing them with other ingredients, so their flexibility is important. A heavy-duty non-stick frying pan and a sharp plastic fish slice make things a great deal easier when you come to do the cooking.

Thin pancakes   *makes about 16*   **2 eggs, plus 1 extra egg yolk   225g flour   pinch of salt   100 ml milk 100ml water 1 teaspoon melted butter, plus more for cooking**

Whisk the eggs and extra yolk into the flour, add the salt and stir in the milk with the same volume of water along with the melted butter. You are aiming for the consistency of thick cream; depending on your flour, you may need to add a little more or less water.

Buttermilk pancakes   *makes about 12*   **2 eggs, plus 1 extra yolk   225g flour   1 dessertspoon sugar pinch of salt   200ml buttermilk   scant half teaspoon baking soda, sieved   butter, for frying**

Whisk the eggs and extra yolk into the flour, add the sugar and salt and stir in the buttermilk along with the melted butter and baking powder and a little extra water if required. You are aiming for a consistency similar to whipped cream; in other words, thicker than the batter above. Depending on your flour, you may need to add a little more or less water. Test by spooning a little of the batter into a lightly oiled frying pan, it should hold its shape well.

Heat a suitable pan lightly brushed with oil and, when hot, pour in just enough batter depending on the size you require. Cook for 1-2 minutes until bubbles appear on top. Flip over and cook the other side until browned. As you cook them, keep the pancakes warm piled on a plate in a warm oven for up to 30 minutes.

Crispy pancetta and maple syrup   **1 quantity Buttermilk pancake batter   200g pancetta maple syrup to serve**

Cook the buttermilk pancakes and keep warm as above.

The nearest to fail-safe method to crisp up pancetta and bacon is to lay it in a shallow, lightly oiled roasting tray and place in an oven preheated to 200°C/gas mark 6 for 8 minutes, or until crisped up. Serve on top of a pile of pancakes with lots of maple syrup.

Toasted muffins may seem old-fashioned but who is complaining?
Thickly spread with golden yellow butter they sooth and comfort
like nothing else

Bagels and muffins

For a proper bagel the dough is first poached in boiling water, a step that is too often overlooked but which is responsible for that unmistakable crusty smooth crust. Toasted muffins make ideal hot sandwiches. The toasting is essential, otherwise they can taste too doughy.

Toasted bagels with cream cheese, red onion and smoked salmon

**4 bagels   6 tablespoons cream cheese   1 small red onion, peeled and cut into thin half-moon slices
200g smoked salmon   1 lemon**

Halve the bagels, toast them and spread with cream cheese. Scatter a few slices of onion over each bottom half. Season with salt and pepper, top with the smoked salmon and squeeze over a little lemon juice. Spread the remaining bagel halves with cream cheese and place them on top.

If you are reluctant about the red onion component, place the cut onion in a sieve and work a teaspoon of salt in with your fingers. Leave for 5 minutes and then rinse under plenty of cold running water, squeezing gently. Use as above. This treatment lessens the power of the onion a little.

Other combinations for toasted bagels
Hummus, rocket and roasted peppers   Smoked chicken, guacamole and brie
Emmental, pastrami and Avoca cucumber relish   Ham, cream cheese and chives
Rare roast beef, horseradish and cherry tomatoes

Suggestions for toasted muffin fillings:
Caramelised red onion, Parma crisps (see page 118) and bleu d'Auvergne   Ham, coleslaw and mustard
Grilled tomatoes and anchovies   Sautéed mushrooms with garlic and parsley

To caramelise red onions, peel and cut into thin half-moon slices. Heat 3 tablespoons of olive oil in a frying pan and add four onions. Season with salt and pepper, scatter over a tablespoon of sugar and a tablespoon of balsamic vinegar. Cook over a moderate heat for 15-20 minutes, or until the onions caramelise.

Sandwiches and melts

Good-quality bread is essential. You want its texture and flavour to work with the other ingredients. Don't slice it too thickly or the bread will soon overpower. Keep to a theme, a magpie approach only leads to confusion.

In essence melts are a posh slant on cheese on toast, the object being to melt or soften the ingredients so they become one (more or less). The bread can vary, from ciabatta to foccacia, cheese soda bread, brown soda bread and straight yeast bread. Toast your chosen bread, spread it with the ingredients, top with the cheese and then warm through in the oven until the cheese just melts.

Sandwich suggestions

Cold roast lamb with mint sauce, tarragon and crème fraîche

Beef, horseradish, mascarpone, crispy onions, rocket, roasted red peppers

Shredded goose, red cabbage, mayonnaise and Greek yoghurt, sliced apple tossed in lemon juice and toasted pumpkin seeds

BLT – grilled smoked Gubbeen bacon, slow-roasted tomatoes, mayonnaise, rocket, watercress, Cos lettuce and black mustard seeds soaked in a little lemon juice for 20 minutes

Melt suggestions

Tuna, corn, mayonnaise and chives, mature cheddar and caramelised red onions (see bottom of page 71)

Grilled red peppers (see page 40) and goat's cheese

Pesto, roast Mediterranean vegetables and buffalo mozzarella

Mushroom à la crème, smoked chicken and blanched asparagus and brie

Making pesto is not difficult and tasting is required to get the balance of ingredients correct. The following is a guide line. 1 large bunch of basil, 75g grated parmesan, 50g pine nuts, 1 garlic clove mashed with a little salt, 150ml of olive oil. Blitz in a processor and season with salt and pepper to taste.

Beef, horseradish, mascarpone, crispy onions, rocket and roasted red pepper sandwich

Kedgeree

Basmati rice may be traditional, but brown rice introduces a delicious nuttiness to the finished dish. If you want to use basmati, as we have done in the picture, reduce the cooking time by 10 minutes and start tasting then.

600g smoked haddock

1.1 litres milk and water mixed

125g butter

1 onion, finely chopped

225g brown rice

2 heaped tablespoons chopped parsley

4 cardamom seeds

1 dessertspoon garam masala

1 teaspoon ground coriander

1 teaspoon cumin seeds

4 cloves

1 dessertspoon chopped fresh ginger

1 green chilli, seeds removed and finely chopped

2 bay leaves

2 hard-boiled eggs

Put the bay leaves into the milk and water mixture and add the fish which has had the skin removed. Bring to a simmer and poach for 5 minutes. Strain and keep the liquid and the fish separately.

Melt 70g of the butter and when hot add all the spices; cook for one minute and add the onion, chilli and ginger and cook for a further 5 minutes. Add the rice and stir to coat; stir-fry for three minutes.

Cover the rice mixture with the strained milk and water and simmer for 30-40 minutes until the rice is cooked but retains a nutty texture. Drain well and then fork through the remaining butter in small pieces, the parsley and the smoked fish, broken into bite size pieces. Add some salt and pepper if necessary.

Divide the hard boiled eggs into 4 and gently stir into the kedgeree. Serve hot

Cooking rice is not an exact science. Adding it to boiling water is certainly a more straightforward method, but the method above allows for an exchange of flavours. The rice's age, provenance and storing conditions all affect both its flavour and its cooking time. As does the power of your cooker. You need to taste as you cook, keeping in mind the rice will go on cooking when you turn the heat off.

Mixed berry and cinnamon scone

This is a delicious twist on an essentially classic food. We are very inclined to stick with conventional scones, but different fruits, even savoury versions (see page 78) make for wonderful twists on familiar themes. The preparation time is short and they cook quite quickly.

450g flour, plus more for dusting
50g caster sugar
1 heaped teaspoon baking powder
quarter teaspoon cinnamon
pinch of salt
110g butter, cubed
1 egg
200ml milk
blueberries, sliced strawberries, redcurrants (you can also use dried cranberries and bilberries as well as raspberries, but the latter tend to bleed). Frozen fruit does not work in this recipe as there is too much liquid.

Preheat the oven to 200°C/gas mark 6. Mix all the dry ingredients together in a bowl with a pinch of salt. Add the butter and, using your fingertips, lightly work until the mix resembles dry breadcrumbs. Add the egg, fruit and just enough milk to moisten (you want a reasonably dry mixture). Mix well until you achieve a soft doughy texture that is not too moist.

Gather into a ball and turn on to a floured surface. Roll lightly to a depth of 1.5cm for baby scones, or 3cm thickness for the larger version and cut out using a 3-5cm cutter or 7cm cutter. Bake in the preheated oven for 10-12 minutes for baby scones or 18-20 minutes for the more conventional sized version, or until cooked.

Breakfast butter bean salad

A plate or two of cured meat and salami is a great way to broaden the range of food on offer with minimal input from the cook. This salad makes for a great accompaniment.

200g dried butter beans, soaked overnight in plenty of cold water
6 tablespoons extra virgin olive oil, plus more to serve
4 garlic cloves, crushed with a little salt
2 red chillies, finely chopped, or to taste
1 tablespoon roughly chopped semi-sun-dried tomatoes
1 teaspoon finely chopped rosemary

Rinse the soaked beans in plenty of water, drain and cover with fresh water. Cook until tender, the time depends on the age of your beans but should be somewhere around 45 minutes. Simmer rather than boil, otherwise the skin is inclined to separate from the bean.

Drain and, while still hot, stir in the olive oil, garlic and chillies. Stir so everything is amalgamated. It is important to do this while the beans are warm, so they absorb the flavours. When the salad has cooled add the sun-dried tomatoes and rosemary. Season with salt and pepper. You may need to dress the beans with more oil when serving. You can also add chunks of feta and pitted black olives.

Baby cheese and sun-dried tomato scones

These savoury scones are great with slices of vine-ripened tomatoes, buffalo mozzarella and coffee.

makes about 12

450g flour, plus more for dusting
1 heaped teaspoon baking powder
small pinch cayenne pepper
generous pinch of salt
110g butter, cubed
1 egg
about 200ml milk
50g grated mature cheddar
8 semi-sun-dried tomatoes, chopped
8 pitted black olives, roughly chopped

Preheat the oven to 200°C/gas mark 6. Mix all the dry ingredients together in a bowl with a generous pinch of salt. Add the butter and, using your fingertips, lightly work until the mix resembles dry breadcrumbs. Stir in the grated cheddar, semi-sun-dried tomatoes and the olives. Make a well in the centre and add the egg and just enough milk to moisten (you want a reasonably dry mixture). Gather into a ball and turn on to a floured surface. Roll lightly to a 1.5cm thickness, cut out as many scones as you can with a 3-4cm cutter and bake in the oven for 10-12 minutes, or until cooked.

SALADS

Whether it is a simple rocket salad dressed with little more than good olive oil, lemon juice and a sprinkling of shaved Pecorino or Parmesan; or a more composed salad of duck confit with frisée, lentils and crisp potatoes, we seem to delight in this ancient food. It is the Romans who are responsible for these diverse and endlessly variable dishes.

In the cafés, we offer literally hundreds of salads through the year, from the more winter-based likes of celeriac rémoulade through to summer-herb dressed leaves and much in between. So fond are customers of salads that many opt for salads and nothing else.

Bowls are generally large and the person composing the salad needs restraint. If you are not careful, too many elements are combined and the overall effect is confusing. Limit your ingredients and make them work together. Colour is vital, so too is texture. Variety is essential, and the range of leaves now available means your salad bowl can run from dark red through green to yellow.

Salads are a great way to start a meal, their colour immediately inviting. Generally light and easy to eat, they leave guests keen for their next course, always a good sign.

Salads receive a blast of early summer sun at Organic Life farm, Kilpedder, Co Wicklow

Spiced chickpea salad

Chickpeas are probably the favourite pulse, judging by customers' reactions to the salads we produce using this versatile ingredient. Something about their nutty sweetness is the attraction, perhaps.

1 onion, finely chopped
4 tablespoons olive oil, plus more to dress
3cm piece of root ginger, grated
1 red chilli, finely chopped
2 teaspoons curry powder
1 teaspoon ground cumin
1 teaspoon ground coriander
pinch of turmeric
2 teaspoons black onion seeds
4 garlic cloves
1 x 400g tin of tomatoes
3 x 400g tins of chickpeas, rinsed and drained
bunch of fresh coriander, roughly chopped
bunch of chives, roughly chopped
bunch of flat-leaf parsley, roughly chopped

Gently sauté the onion in the olive oil for 10-15 minutes without allowing it to colour. Add all the spices, chilli and the garlic and cook for 2 minutes. Add the tomatoes and reduce on a low heat for 15-20 minutes, stirring occasionally. Dress the chickpeas in this sauce while it is still warm. Allow to cool, then add the herbs (this stops them discolouring) and drizzle over more olive oil.

In the cafés we always use dried pulses, soaking them overnight in several changes of water and then cooking them in a large volume of water. This process helps to rid them of the elements that sometimes make them difficult to digest. For small numbers, however, tins are well worth considering. And brands do matter, international ones generally being surpassed by those from countries fond of pulses. Italy, Spain and France spring to mind, but so too do most Mediterranean countries. If cost is a concern, consider that the difference between a national Spanish brand and say an international one is a few pence.

Spiced cannellini bean and tomato salad

175g dried cannellini beans, soaked overnight
5 tablespoons olive oil
pinch of turmeric
quarter teaspoon ground cumin
half teaspoon black onion seeds
generous grinding of black pepper
2 red chillies, deseeded and finely diced
3 garlic cloves, crushed
100g coarsely chopped semi-sun-dried tomatoes
bunch of fresh coriander, stalks chopped finely, leaves roughly (or alternatively a bunch of parsley)
bunch of mint, leaves picked and roughly chopped
juice of 1 lemon

Drain the beans and rinse well. Cover with fresh water, bring to the boil, skim the froth and simmer gently for an hour or until cooked. The time they take really does depend on how old they are. As pulses age they toughen up, so really old examples will need as long as 3 hours to cook. Better to buy anew. This stage can be done in advance, but if you do this you need to reheat them in boiling water and drain before adding the oil, so they are warm.

Gently warm the olive oil in a frying pan and add the dried spices, chillies and garlic and stir over a moderate heat for 2 minutes. When the beans are cooked, drain well and mix with the warm olive oil mixture. Allow to cool to room temperature.

Add the semi-sun-dried tomatoes, coriander or parsley, mint, lemon juice and season well. You need to add the herbs once the mixture has cooled so they keep their colour.

Variations   the spiced cannellini beans go well with lamb: a few chops, a rack, or a whole leg. They also make another good salad when cooked and combined with finely diced red pepper, chopped fresh plum tomatoes, lots of finely chopped parsley, chopped garlic and olive oil with a squeeze of lemon.

There is nothing wrong with tinned pulses, provided you buy a good brand - Italian and Spanish tend to be the best. After all, pulses have been sold in European markets for hundreds of years, cooked by the stall-holder and served by the spoonful. Remember to rinse off the liquid surrounding tinned pulses.

Confit of duck, frisée, lentils and crisp potatoes

This robust salad is inspired by the cooking of the south west of France. The confit recipe is given on page 204. In this salad, the meat is used at room temperature.

Walnut oil has a tendency to go rancid quite quickly; once opened it will keep for longer if stored in the fridge. This makes it solidify, but once brought back to room temperature it will become clear and liquid again.

175g Puy lentils
1 carrot, finely diced
1 celery stick, finely diced
2 garlic cloves, finely chopped
8 tablespoons olive oil
4 teaspoons balsamic vinegar
1 teaspoon fresh thyme
2 large waxy potatoes, peeled and cut into 2cm dice
about 8 tablespoons olive oil
1 head of frisée, trimmed and washed
2 tablespoons walnut oil
4 confit duck legs, shredded (see page 204)
handful of toasted walnuts
chervil or flat-leaf parsley to garnish

Preheat the oven to 200°C/gas mark 6. Wash the lentils in several changes of cold water, cover with fresh water, bring to the boil and simmer for 10-15 minutes, or until cooked but still with bite, adding the diced carrot and celery for the final 5 minutes.

Drain and combine with the garlic, half the olive oil, 3 teaspoons of balsamic vinegar and the thyme, stirring so everything is well mixed. Season with salt and pepper.

Toss the cubed potato in the remaining olive oil, season with salt and pepper and roast in the preheated oven for 10-15 minutes, or until golden and tender.

Toss the frisée with the walnut oil and the remaining teaspoon of balsamic vinegar and season with salt and pepper. Pile in the centre of 4 plates, making each one as high as possible. Top with shredded confit and spoon the lentils and potatoes around the plate with a few walnuts. Garnish with chervil or flat-leaf parsley.

Seared fillet of beef, spiced roast potatoes and rocket

This is a very popular way with beef throughout Italy, highlighting this meat's delicacy. Light white or red wine should accompany, rather than anything too full-bodied.

2 garlic cloves, finely chopped

2 fresh kaffir lime leaves, finely shredded

2 teaspoons cumin seeds

50ml soy sauce

450g fillet of beef in one piece

500g new potatoes, cubed

about 250ml extra virgin olive oil

3 star anise

2 teaspoons sweet smoked paprika

1 teaspoon fennel seeds

50ml lime juice

1 teaspoon ground coriander seeds

4 tablespoons sesame oil

4 large handfuls of rocket

1 teaspoon balsamic vinegar, plus more for sprinkling

Combine the first 4 ingredients with the meat, toss gently, cover with cling film and set aside for a few hours, overnight is better.

Preheat the oven to 200°C/gas mark 6. Toss the potatoes with 150ml of the olive oil, the star anise, paprika, fennel, lime juice, coriander seeds, sesame oil and 125 ml water in a roasting pan. Roast for 20-25 minutes in the preheated oven, until golden and crispy, turning twice.

Turn the oven up to 220°C/gas mark 7. Brush the marinade off the meat, coat it lightly in olive oil and seal in an ovenproof pan. Transfer to the oven and roast for 10 minutes (rare) to 15 minutes (well done), depending on taste. Allow to rest for 5 minutes and slice thinly.

Dress the rocket with a teaspoon of balsamic vinegar and 3 tablespoons of olive oil. Season well with salt and pepper. Scatter the potatoes on the bottom of each plate, pile the rocket on top, arrange the slices of beef over the leaves and sprinkle with a little more oil and balsamic vinegar.

Variation   Serve this as a sandwich with crispy shallots, roasted red peppers, rocket and crème fraîche mixed with grated horseradish (see picture on page 73).

Tracy salad

Named after Tracy McCormack, this salad combines all the spiciness of the chorizo with the rocket leaves and has been very popular in Suffolk Street from the beginning.

20 thin slices of chorizo, cut at an angle
3 potatoes, peeled and diced
4 tablespoons extra virgin olive oil
1 dessertspoon balsamic vinegar
4 handfuls of rocket
8 semi-sun-dried tomatoes
225g feta, cubed

Preheat the oven to 180°C/gas mark 4. Lay the chorizo slices out on a shallow baking tray and dry bake in the oven until crisp, about 20 minutes. Cook the potatoes in boiling salted water until tender. Drain well and toss with salt and pepper, the olive oil and balsamic vinegar. Toss the potatoes with the rocket and add the chorizo, along with any oil that has gathered in the roasting tray. Scatter over the sun-dried tomatoes and feta and serve.

Thai chicken salad

This salad can also be made with fillet of pork, prawns or monkfish, for example. Toasting the peanuts may seem like rather a lot of work, but it really is worth the extra trouble – ready salted nuts just don't compare.

Skewers are less likely to burn if they are soaked in cold water for an hour or two before use. Additionally, you can cover the ends with a little foil, which prevents blackened points.

2 skinless chicken breasts
1 jar of good-quality satay sauce
2 tablespoons monkey nuts
4 handfuls of beansprouts
1 handful of mange tout, thinly sliced
1 red pepper, thinly sliced
2 pak choi, shredded
4 spring onions, sliced at an angle
1 garlic clove, finely chopped and then mashed with a little salt
1 teaspoon grated ginger
2 tablespoons sesame oil, plus more for brushing
1 tablespoon rice wine vinegar or soy sauce
1 tablespoon toasted sesame seeds

Cut the chicken into thin strips, coat these in the satay sauce and thread on to skewers.

Roast the peanuts in an oven preheated to 200°C/gas mark 6 for 10-15 minutes, or until crispy and golden in colour. Don't under-roast them or they will go soft.

In a large bowl, mix all the vegetables, garlic, ginger and roasted nuts. Lightly toss with the sesame oil and rice wine vinegar.

Grill the chicken skewers for 4 minutes on each side, remove from the heat and brush with more sesame oil.

Pile the salad high and criss-cross the chicken satay on top. Sprinkle over the toasted sesame seeds.

Variation   You can include baby corn cobs, but these need to be blanched in boiling salted water until tender before being added to the salad.

Nuts

We use nuts all the time in the cafés, in lots of the salads and in quite a few of the tarts, cakes and sweet things. Despite their hardy appearance, they do not last forever and should be bought in small quantities.

Most nuts can be bought either in the shell or shelled. In addition, quite a few nuts can also be bought blanched, flaked and ground. As a general rule, the greater the surface area, the faster the deterioration through oxidation. The most common incidence of this is when you buy ground almonds which are then not used for months. Your almond flavour will be far better if you grind blanched almonds yourself. Good fresh nuts taste sweet as well as nutty and have a crispness and a full meaty texture.

Walnuts   Useful not only in tarts, cakes and confectionery generally, but also in salads and sauces, the latter particularly with chicken, when walnuts can be mashed to a purée with spices, garlic, herbs and oil.

Peanuts   Often referred to as monkey nuts in their unsalted and unroasted state, these are actually a member of the pea and bean family and not strictly a nut at all. Freshly roasted, they add a rich flavour to dishes, particularly satay, which salted peanuts simply cannot match.

Pistachios   Widely used in the Middle East, these nuts contribute a green colour to foods as diverse as Italian mortadella and Indian kulfi ice-cream. They are also used in nougat and Turkish delight, as well as French terrines.

Pine nuts   Always expensive as they have to be harvested by hand, pine nuts are particularly good when lightly toasted in a dry frying pan or in a little butter to enhance their flavour. We use them widely, particularly tossed over salads. While their role in pesto is widely known, the same recipe can be used incorporating coriander, mint and parsley in place of the basil, for a somewhat different result. They burn incredibly easily.

Almonds   Perhaps the most widely used nut of all, almonds turn up as much in sweet dishes as they do in savoury. If you buy them with their skin on, blanching is simply done by immersing them in boiling water for a few minutes, and the skins then rub off. Almonds are popular in Spanish and Portuguese cooking to thicken and enrich stews and soups.

Pecans   These are native to the US, so it is no surprise that pecan pie is one of this nut's favoured homes. We use them in baking and savoury tarts, a welcome alternative to walnuts.

Hazelnuts   We use hazelnuts extensively, mostly in salads and cakes They are easy to skin; roast in a moderate oven and rub in tea towel.

From the top, left to right: pecans, hazelnuts, pine nuts, almonds, pistachios, walnut pieces, peanuts

Smoked duck, rocket and Parmesan salad

We have seen quite a growth in the number of smokeries around Ireland in recent years. Salmon is possibly the most common ingredient to be smoked, but duck is fast gaining favour. This salad is really quick and easy to prepare, and looks rather more impressive than the sum of its parts might suggest.

6 tablespoons balsamic vinegar
4 large handfuls of rocket
4-6 tablespoons extra virgin olive oil
1 smoked duck breast
25g Parmesan shavings

Reduce the balsamic vinegar in a heavy saucepan over a low heat until thick and syrupy. Allow to cool. Toss the rocket leaves with 4 tablespoons of the olive oil and the reduced balsamic vinegar. Season with salt and pepper. Slice the duck breast as thinly as possible. Pile the dressed rocket in the centre of 4 plates, arrange the duck breast around the edge and sprinkle over the Parmesan.

Variation   This salad also works well with smoked chicken in place of the duck. You can also add toasted pine nuts, which should be dry-fried in a moderately hot frying pan for a scant minute or two.

Carrot and celeriac rémoulade

Rémoulade is a mayonnaise-based sauce used to dress salads and cold meats. Opinions vary about what turns it from mayonnaise into rémoulade, but top of the list are mustard, gherkins, capers and herbs.

1 small celeriac
5 carrots
3 tablespoon mayonnaise
4 tablespoons Greek-style yoghurt
1 heaped teaspoon grainy mustard

Peel the celeriac and carrots and process them to shreds on the julienne blade of your food processor. Combine with the mayonnaise, yoghurt and mustard, and dress the julienned vegetables. Season with salt and pepper.

Baby gem and rocket salad

This is a big-bowl salad, nothing too delicate or fancy.

4 little gem lettuces
4 handfuls of rocket
12 pecans
1 teaspoon Cajun spices
8 slices of streaky bacon
olive oil, for frying
2 tablespoons Greek-style yoghurt
2 tablespoons mayonnaise
100g Roquefort
Croutons (see page 18)

Break the little gems up into individual leaves and put in a bowl along with the rocket. Toss the pecans with the Cajun spices and toast briefly on both sides under the grill. Watch them like a hawk, they will turn from toasted to burnt in seconds.

Cut the bacon into lardons and cook in a lightly oiled frying pan until they crisp up. Remove and drain on kitchen paper. Combine the yoghurt, mayonnaise, half the Roquefort and season. Blitz in a blender and add a little water if too thick. Mix the dressing with the leaves and half the bacon, croutons and pecans and season with salt and pepper. Pile the salad on to 4 plates and sprinkle the remaining ingredients on top.

Mayonnaise   2 egg yolks   300ml good-quality vegetable oil   lemon juice to taste

It helps considerably if all your ingredients and equipment are at room temperature. In a bowl, season the egg yolks with salt. Whisking vigorously, add the oil drop by drop initially, until the mixture emulsifies and forms a thick heavy paste. At this point you can increase the stream of oil to a steady trickle, continuing to whisk. Add a little of the lemon juice as the sauce thickens. Once all the oil is incorporated adjust the seasoning and add more lemon juice if appropriate. If the mixture splits, start again with a fresh yolk adding the split mixture as you did the oil.

Making mayonnaise is easier than many think and can be done in a mixer, particularly useful for larger quantities. It will keep happily in the fridge for a week or two. The key item to watch is your eggs, which need to be the freshest possible.

Pea, pancetta, broad bean and goat's cheese salad

At the height of summer it is often the most simple of foods that are the best. If you have a garden full of fresh peas, so much the better; for most, however, the certainty of frozen peas is a blessing. Broad beans, too, come frozen, but still need to be skinned.

400g fresh broad beans, podded (about 1kg of beans in their pods)
8 slices of pancetta
400g frozen peas
1 garlic clove, finely chopped
150g goat's cheese
juice of 1 lemon
2 tablespoons extra virgin olive oil, plus more to serve
1 large bunch of fresh mint, finely chopped

Blanch the broad beans in boiling salted water for 1 minute, drain and refresh. Remove the skins and discard.

Preheat the oven to 220°C/gas mark 7. Lay the pancetta on a shallow baking sheet and bake for 10-20 minutes (watch it after the first 10 minutes as pancetta and ovens vary widely).

Blanch the peas in boiling water for 2 minutes, or until just cooked.

Mash the garlic into the goat's cheese and season with salt and pepper and lemon juice. Toss the broad beans and peas in 2 tablespoons of olive oil. Crumble the goat's cheese over the peas and broad beans and sprinkle over the mint.

Spoon on to 4 plates, top with a couple of slices of crispy pancetta and spoon over a little more olive oil. Sprinkle with black pepper and serve.

Niçoise with slow-roasted tuna loin

Fresh tuna is a world away from its tinned cousins. It has a taste of the sea and a sweet meatiness unlike any other fish. Take care when cooking; for such dense flesh it cooks in no time.

500g tuna loin in a piece
2 garlic cloves, smashed
8 black peppercorns
about 250ml olive oil
200g French beans
1 large Cos lettuce, separated
juice of half a lemon
450g new potatoes, halved
dash of red wine vinegar
2 tablespoons pitted black olives
8 semi-sun-dried tomatoes or good cherry tomatoes
12 marinated sweet anchovies
4 eggs, hard-boiled

Place the tuna in a saucepan and add the garlic, peppercorns and sea salt. Pour in enough olive oil to cover and bring slowly to the boil, turn off the heat and leave to cool. The tuna will keep for a week in the fridge and actually improves over that time, as the flavours amalgamate.

Cook the potatoes in the same water as the beans, drain and toss with 3 tablespoons of olive oil, the red wine vinegar and a seasoning of salt and pepper.

Blanch the French beans in salted water for 4 minutes or until cooked but still al dente. While they are still warm, combine with the lettuce in a bowl and season with salt and pepper. Add 3 tablespoons of olive oil and the lemon juice. Toss so everything is well coated.

Spoon the beans and lettuce on to 4 plates, scatter over the potatoes, olives, semi-sun-dried tomatoes and anchovies, and place two egg halves strategically on top. Gently break up the tuna fish and scatter over the other ingredients.

TARTS

Few dishes can so successfully bridge the gap between dyed-in-the-wool traditional and fantastically modern – the tart has finally come of age. In the cafés, we cook tarts every day and rather a lot of them, both sweet and savoury. They can be as homely and old-fashioned as quiche or as up-to-date as strawberry and mascarpone. The Italian influence comes in the shape of slow-roasted plum tomatoes and mozzarella, but we also do more unusual tarts like smoked chicken, pear, pecan and blue cheese.

What goes into a tart really is a matter of preference, but there are a few rules worth thinking about. Three, at the most four, ingredients really is the limit, otherwise everything starts to cancel each other out. This is certainly not the time to use up leftovers if leftovers involve a big clearout of the fridge.

Be influenced by the seasons, they are more of a help than a hindrance. Asparagus is a joy in the summer and not much use to anybody in the winter – and you spoil any sense of anticipation. Quality of ingredients is paramount and pretty much everything grown locally is more likely to taste delicious than something flown in from the other side of the world.

Tarts are not nearly as time-consuming as people fear and, as for resting pastry, would that we could in the cafés; pressure of time means we cannot. This raises an interesting question however. Why do we rest pastry in the first place?

The main reason is to prevent shrinkage, a process that occurs as the pastry cooks and the gluten, which you have stretched, shrinks back. This is not a huge problem to overcome; you simply need to leave enough of an overlap at the edge that can be trimmed after the tart has been baked.

A note on sizing

In the cafés, tarts are made in 28cm tart shells, which we reckon makes for somewhere between 8 and 12 servings, depending on how deep the filling is. Here we have specified a deep 23cm tart tin which, depending on hunger levels as well as fillings and what is served with it, will feed 6-8 people. The tins are loose-bottomed, which makes the tarts far easier to extract..

Baking blind

In the café kitchens we bake up to 20 tart bases at a time. All are baked blind to ensure the pastry remains crisp after it has been filled. This is the procedure

It is important to preheat the oven. The objective is to dry the pastry out and firm up the shape so not only is there no leakage, but the pastry does not become moist with the filling. The cooking time to achieve this is between 20 and 30 minutes.

You need to line the pastry with paper to prevent the beans from sticking to it. Greaseproof paper is fine, but it does tend to go brittle in the oven and disintegrate. Bakewell paper is more supple and ensures the edges do not collapse.

The base needs to be weighed down so it doesn't rise off the base of the tin. You can buy ceramic beans to weigh down on top of the pastry and, although quite expensive, these will last you for ever. In the kitchen we use dry butter beans, which after a time are replaced with new ones.

It is hard to be more precise than this; the variables are your oven, the flour you use, even the moisture on the day will effect the cooking time of your tart base. You will need to experiment a little and don't forget that the top, untrimmed edges will go brown even when the tart base is still pale. You will be trimming off these top edges, so don't worry about them.

When you remove the base from the oven, leave it on the side for 10 minutes to allow everything to settle down. If your filling is very moist, remove the paper and the beans and egg-wash the pastry; brush with lightly beaten whole egg and return to the oven for 5 minutes. At this stage you can get shrinkage and air bubbles creeping in. Allow the shell to cool completely in the tin.

Roll out the pastry so it will be at least 4cm proud of the edge of the tin once it is pressed into the corner. This is to allow for shrinkage and, although it looks quite alarming going into the oven, is necessary. It will be trimmed off later.

There are a number of different recipes for tart cases. The first is a basic, foolproof any-one-can-do pastry. The next introduces more fat and reduces the water content to give a more crumbly and crispy texture and flavour. Wholewheat gives a more robust base for certain savoury fillings and you can then introduce seeds and flavourings to complement the fillings. For sweet tarts, we increase the egg yolk and sugar content even further and start to introduce ground nuts for richness and flavour.

Puff pastry
Hardly anybody – bar very grand restaurants and lunatics like Fleur Campbell – makes puff pastry. Go to the supermarket and buy it. The quality of puff pastry does vary however, so experiment. The cheaper brands make extensive use of hydrogenated vegetable oil.

Lightness
As any experienced cook will tell you, the art (as opposed to the science) of making pastry is all in the hands. Lightness of touch, a certain coolness to the hands is what separates the good from the outstanding. In a real sense, you either have it or you don't, but the only way you will discover is by trying. Everybody can make good pastry, the cold hands are the ones making exceptional pastry.

Tough pastry
This is caused by overworking the dough, which toughens up the gluten. A light hand is required, once everything has come together, leave well alone.

Food processor
You can use a food processor, but we wouldn't recommend it initially, as a lot of care is required to avoid the pastry being tough. If you are determined, use sparingly and don't over-process.

Patching
If you end up with gaps these can be plugged using more raw pastry. They should be 'glued' in place with egg wash, which avoids any leakage.

A general note on seasoning
It is a good idea to season each of the main ingredients before you assemble the filling. So, for example, with smoked salmon, dill and asparagus tart, both the salmon and the asparagus should be seasoned before they are combined.

Avoiding soggy pastry
Soggy pastry generally results from a liquid filling leaking into the pastry before it has had a chance to set. See baking blind (page 104) for ways to avoid this.

Savoury base one   *makes a 23cm pastry case (serves 6-8)*   **350g plain flour   175g butter   1 egg   half teaspoon salt**

Combine all the ingredients and add just enough cold water (a tablespoon or three) to form a dough. More cold water will make the pastry easier to roll, but increases the shrinkage when baked.

Savoury base two   *makes a 23cm pastry case (serves 6-8)*   **350g plain flour   225g butter   4 egg yolks   half teaspoon salt**

Combine all the ingredients and add just enough cold water to form a dough (1-2 tablespoons).

Savoury base three (wholewheat)   *makes a 23cm pastry case (serves 6-8)*   **175g plain flour   175g wholemeal flour   200g butter   2 whole eggs   half teaspoon salt**

Combine all the ingredients and add just enough cold water to form a dough (1-2 tablespoons).

Cheese and chilli   Both cheese and chilli provide variations, the cheese bringing a richness and the chilli helping to cut some of the richer fillings. Don't overdo it, however, you don't want the pastry to overpower the filling. If you are using cheese you must use a quality mature Cheddar (or similar) or you'll never taste it. If using chilli, you can use chilli flakes, Tabasco or a pinch of cayenne.

Basic sweet shortcrust   *makes a 25cm pastry case (serves 8-10)*   **225g plain flour   150g butter   25g caster sugar   1-2 egg yolks**

Rub the flour and butter together, stir in the caster sugar and make a well in the centre. Add the egg yolks and just enough water to form a ball with the flour mixture. Wrap in cling film and leave to rest in the fridge.

Preheat the oven to 190°C/gas mark 5. Roll out the pastry and use to line a 25cm fluted deep-flan case. Bake blind for 25 minutes. Generally, we would now paint the base with egg wash and return to the oven for 5 minutes to seal.

Chocolate pastry   Add a dessertspoon of cocoa powder to the basic sweet shortcrust and add an additional 15g of caster sugar.

Quiches

Classic combinations include ham and cheese, spinach and pine nuts or asparagus and Parmesan. Good eggs are essential. Restraint is also necessary; if you add too many ingredients, they start to cancel each other out.

The idea is to combine the fillings with a custard and then bake the finished tart. The second custard recipe below is a little less rich in that it uses less cream but it is more eggy than the first.

for custard 1
350ml cream
3 eggs, plus 2 extra yolks

for custard 2
175ml cream
175ml milk
5 eggs, plus 2 extra yolks

Suggested fillings
cooked smoked bacon, gently sautéed leeks and mature Cheddar   baby spinach, Parmesan, pine nuts and black olives   horseradish smoked trout and watercress

Smoked salmon, dill and asparagus tart

You can use the off-cuts of salmon in this tart. They are certainly cheaper, but they do also tend to be slightly fatty and for that reason we don't use them in the cafés.

450g smoked salmon, roughly chopped (this sounds like a lot and is well worth it - you can get away with using 350g)   1 tablespoon chopped dill   custard one or two (see above)   1 pastry case, baked blind (see page 109)   8 blanched and refreshed asparagus spears

Preheat the oven to 160°C/gas mark 3. Add the smoked salmon and dill to your chosen custard, season with salt and pepper and pour into the pastry base. Bake in the preheated oven for 25 minutes.

Gently remove from the oven and place the asparagus like spokes of a wheel on top. Return to the oven for a further 20 minutes, or until just set.

Slow-roasted plum tomato and mozzarella tart

5 ripe plum tomatoes, cored and cut in half lengthways   2 buffalo mozzarella   1 pastry case, baked blind (see page 109)   8 basil leaves   8 pitted black olives   custard one or two

Place the tomatoes on a shallow baking sheet, season with salt and pepper and a little sugar. Bake in a preheated oven, 170°C/gas mark 3 for 1.5 hours, remove and pour off the excess moisture. Leave the tomatoes on kitchen paper to soak up any excess moisture and intensify the flavour.

Slice the mozzarella and intersperse with the tomatoes in a circle round the tart. Scatter over the olives. Tear four of the basil leaves and lay on top. Pour in the custard and bake in a low oven, 150°C/gas mark 2 for 40 minutes, or until set. Don't worry if it has a wobble on it when it comes out, it will set as it cools.

Variation   Instead of the plum tomatoes use a punnet of cherry tomatoes, or half yellow and half red, two tablespoons pitted black olives and small chunks of feta.

Smoked chicken, pear, pecan and blue cheese tart

Cashel Blue works particularly well in this recipe, but other creamy blue cheeses, like Bleu d'Auvergne can be substituted. Avoid using a Stilton, however, as it tends to dry out and go crumbly when it is cooked.

4 ripe pears, peeled, cored and halved (in the cafés we use good quality tinned pears)   110g Cashel Blue cheese
1 pastry case, baked blind (see page 109)   2 smoked chicken breasts, sliced lengthways
1 dessertspoon chopped tarragon   custard one or two   8 halved pecans

Preheat the oven to 150°C/gas mark 2 and eat one of the pear halves. Spoon a little of the blue cheese into each hollow in the remaining seven pear halves. Lay the pears in the pastry crust, cut side down, with one in the centre. Intersperse with the smoked chicken.

Stir the tarragon into the custard and pour into the shell. Cook in the preheated oven for 25 minutes. Remove, put the pecans on top, with two in the centre, and return to the oven for a further 20 minutes, or until just set.

Smoked haddock, leek and Cheddar tart

350g smoked haddock

600ml full-fat milk

1 bay leaf

1 blade of mace

300ml cream

pinch of saffron

2 medium leeks, trimmed, cut lengthways and thinly sliced

50g butter

75g flour

4 potatoes, peeled, diced and cooked in boiling salted water until tender

1 pastry case, baked blind (see page 109)

2 tablespoons grated Parmesan

1 dessertspoon snipped chives

Preheat the oven to 160°C/gas mark 2. Poach the fish in the milk with the bay leaf and mace for 8-10 minutes, or until it flakes easily. Remove from the milk and allow to cool on a plate. Discard half the milk and combine the rest with the cream and the saffron.

Gently sauté the leeks in the butter for 8-10 minutes, then stir in the flour and cook for 2 minutes. Add the milk and cream mixture, and carry on cooking, stirring continuously for a further 5 minutes.

Flake the haddock and add to the sauce along with the potatoes, and spread in the bottom of your pastry case. Sprinkle over the Parmesan and bake in the preheated oven for 40 minutes, or until set. Scatter over the chives and serve.

Smoked haddock generally comes in two guises, bright yellow, or dusty pink. The first has been dyed as well as smoked, the latter is simply smoked with no additional dye. Unless you like eating artificial colouring, the dusty pink version is the one to go for.

Seasoning tarts: Season everything as you go, including layers. Sprinkle salt from your finger tips about 30cm above the food. Does the height make a difference? It ensures the whole dish is seasoned, rather than an isolated pocket.

Crab, coriander and chilli tart

Crab is one of the sweetest of shellfish. Unlike lobster, so often held to be superior, crab has a succulence that is hard to beat and it is wonderfully versatile. Try tossing cooked crab meat with spaghetti or linguine, a little chilli and some lemon juice and zest for a quick mid-week supper. You need nothing more than salad to follow.

500g cooked and picked, mainly white, fresh crab meat
Tabasco
pinch of mace
1 teaspoon Dijon mustard
3 eggs, separated
250ml crème fraîche
2 tablespoons grated Parmesan
bunch of coriander, stems and leaves chopped
1 pastry case, baked blind (see page 109)

Preheat the oven to 180°C/gas mark 4. Combine the crab meat, a generous slug of Tabasco to taste, the mace, mustard, egg yolks, crème fraîche, Parmesan and coriander. Season well with salt and pepper, remembering the egg whites and pastry will level the seasoning slightly.

Whisk the egg whites until stiff and then fold into the crab mixture. Pour into the tart base and bake in a preheated oven for 30 minutes. Keep an eye on things towards the end; you may need to cover the tart with tin foil to stop it over-browning.

To cook a medium-sized crab drop into boiling salted water for 15 minutes, remove and allow to cool. To crack open, bring the rear edge of the crab sharply down on a work surface and separate the body from the shell. Remove the 'dead man's fingers', which are attached to the main body. Scoop out the brown meat from the main shell. Crack the claws and scoop out the white meat. The main body should be cut in half with a sharp knife, there is plenty of white meat inside but it needs patience to scoop it all out. Crab is often available from harbours with small fishing boats, like Bullock harbour in Dalkey

Mediterranean vegetable and tapenade tart

2 large onions, halved and thinly sliced
about 100ml olive oil
6 large garlic cloves, crushed
2 x 400g tins of chopped tomatoes
glass of red wine
pinch of sugar
1 dessertspoon each of picked marjoram and oregano, plus some extra sprigs for garnish
2 red peppers
1 yellow pepper
1 aubergine
2 courgettes
50g semi-sun-dried tomatoes
1 tablespoon good quality tapenade
1 pastry case, baked blind (see page 104)

Preheat the oven to 200°C/gas mark 6. Gently sauté the onions in 4 tablespoons of olive oil for 10 minutes, or until opaque. Add the garlic, cook for 1 minute and then add the tomatoes, wine and a pinch of sugar. Cook on a low heat until reduced by two-thirds. Stir in most of the herbs. Season with salt and pepper, which is done at this point because of reducing the sauce; add it earlier and you can easily end up overseasoning. You don't need all the sauce for this tart, but the remainder is absolutely delicious on pasta, or on crostini or bruschetta and keeps in the fridge for three to four days.

Cut the vegetables into small dice and toss in olive oil so they are lightly coated. Combine the peppers and aubergines, spread out on a shallow baking tray and roast in the preheated oven for 15 minutes. Remove from the oven and place the courgettes on the tray and return to the oven for barely 5 minutes. Drain all the vegetables, mix together and season. Add the semi-sun-dried tomatoes.

Spread the tapenade over the pastry base, cover with 4 tablespoons of the tomato sauce, scatter over the vegetables. Sprinkle with the sprigs of marjoram and oregano and serve. If you want to enrich the tart further, lay slices of feta, goat's cheese or mozzarella on top and flash under a grill to melt slightly.

Sautéing onions is one of the fundamentals of cooking. Onions contain sugars and if cooked gently and for sufficiently long - somewhere between 10 and 20 minutes - these sugars are drawn out and are responsible for giving the dish a rounded sweetness. Cook the onions too quickly and the sugars burn. Patience at this stage will reward you in the long run.

Strawberry and mascarpone tart
use a 32cm x 12cm rectangular, loose-bottomed tart tin

This is one of the most successful and simple tarts we do. All the summer freshness of strawberries and the richness of mascarpone. The pastry we use for this tart has a lemon flavour and the quantity given matches the size of the tart tin given above.

175g plain flour
100g butter
25g icing sugar
1 egg yolk
zest of half a lemon

Rub the flour and butter together, stir in the caster sugar and lemon zest and make a well in the centre. Add the egg yolk and just enough water to form ball with the flour mixture. Wrap in cling film and leave to rest in the fridge. Roll out to line the tart tin, and bake blind for 15-20 minutes, remove from the oven, extract the beans, egg wash and return to the oven for five minutes. Remove from the oven and allow to cool.

25g caster sugar
275g mascarpone
150ml cream
half vanilla pod, scraped
zest of half an orange
100g strawberry or redcurrant jam
450g fresh strawberries, hulled

Combine the sugar, mascarpone, cream, vanilla seeds and zest. Whisk until it holds its shape, the consistency is similar to lightly whipped cream. In a saucepan, heat the jam with 1 tablespoon of water. Sieve to remove any pips.

Spread the mascarpone filling in the pastry case. Arrange the strawberries in a decorative 'this only took me minutes to do' kind of way. With a pastry brush, glaze the strawberries with the jam mixture.

Summer fruit tartlets

makes 8-10 10cm tartlets

1 quantity Chocolate shortcrust pastry
(page 109)
1 egg, lightly beaten, for the egg wash
100g dark chocolate (melted)
1 quantity crème patisserie
600g mixed summer fruits (blueberries,
raspberries and strawberries for example)
3 tablespoons apricot jam, heated with two
tablespoons of water

for the crème patisserie
250ml milk
250ml cream
75g caster sugar
1 vanilla pod, cut in half and seeds
scraped out
1 egg, plus 3 yolks
40g cornflour

Line the tartlets tins with the pastry and bake blind (see page 109). Remove, egg wash and return to the oven for 5 minutes. Spread the melted chocolate around the inside of the tartlet cases and allow to set.

For the crème patisserie, whisk the whole egg, yolks and caster sugar until pale. Sieve in the cornflour, whisking thoroughly to ensure it is well blended. Heat the milk and cream together with the scraped vanilla pod and the seeds to just below boilng point. Remove the vanilla pod and place in the sugar jar, this flavours your sugar. Add to the egg mixture and whisk. Return to the pan for a further five minutes, whisking continuously until the cornflour has been cooked out and the mixture has thickened. Allow to cool and refrigerate until needed.

Spoon in the crème patisserie and top with the mixed fruit and glaze with the apricot jam.

Rich chocolate tart with mixed berry sorbet

for the mixed berry sorbet
500g frozen mixed berries
125g caster sugar
juice of half lemon
250ml crème fraîche

1 quantity sweet shortcrust pastry (see page 109)

for the chocolate filling
350ml single cream
275g dark chocolate (55 per cent cocoa solids, anything more and it gets too bitter)
1 egg, plus 1 extra egg yolk

Make the sorbet well ahead: defrost the mixed berries and place in a saucepan along with any juice. Add the sugar and heat gently until the sugar has melted and the fruit has softened slightly, about 10 minutes. Leave to cool then push through a sieve. Discard the pulp.

Add the lemon juice to the fruit syrup. Stir in a spoonful of the crème fraîche. Then fold the fruit mixture into the remaining crème fraîche. Pour into an ice-cream machine and churn or, if you don't have one, freeze and beat after 1 1/2 hours and again after 3 hours until set.

Preheat the oven to 180°C/gas mark 4. Roll out the pastry and use to line a 25cm tart tin . Bake blind for 20 minutes in the preheated oven. Remove the baking beans and parchment paper. Egg wash the case and return to the oven for a further 5 minutes. Reduce the oven setting to 140°C/gas mark 1.

Make the filling: heat the cream to just below boiling point. Place the chocolate in a bowl large enough to hold the entire mixture and have enough room to whisk. Pour the heated cream over the chocolate and stir until melted. In a separate bowl, lightly beat the egg and yolk, then whisk this into the chocolate mix. Pour into the pastry case and bake for 30 minutes. Remove when it still has a slight wobble.

Best served within an hour.

Variation   About 75g of homemade praline (see page 211) and a splash of brandy sprinkled over the pastry case before it is filled are quite delicious. Or, try orange zest and a splash of Cointreau.

Pear tarte Tatin

So called because it was apparently invented by the Tatin sisters who ran a small restaurant in rural France, the original tarte uses apples, but pears also work well. Using whole spices - cloves, star anise, or cinnamon, for example - makes an interesting change and helps the finished tart look particularly pretty.

150g unsalted butter
150g caster sugar
4 pears
200g puff pastry
crème fraîche, to serve

Preheat the oven to 180°C/gas mark 4. Smear the butter over the base of a small round ovenproof tin and sprinkle in the sugar. Peel the pears, then core and halve them. Place these, cut side up, on top of the sugar and butter. Place the tin over a moderate heat and cook until the sugar starts to caramelise and turn a darkish brown.

Roll out the pastry and place on top of the pears, don't worry if it sticks out over the edges a bit, simply tuck inside the tin. Transfer to the oven and bake for 30 minutes, or until the pastry is golden brown.

Remove from the oven and allow to cool for about half an hour before turning, pastry side down, on to a plate. Watch out for hot caramelised pear juices. Serve the tart with spoonfuls of crème fraîche.

VEGETABLES

The Italians have taught us so much when it comes to vegetables; think grilled aubergines and peppers, braised fennel, and sautéed potatoes laced with garlic and rosemary.

Yet while aubergines and peppers may be from the Mediterranean, the Italian approach has also made us think about our own native vegetables, like carrots and parsnips, cabbage and broccoli. Where once we boiled them to oblivion, they now turn up roasted and braised, flavoured with anchovies and Parmesan, or simmered in cream and butter.

The dishes in this chapter range from old favourites – macaroni cheese, aloo gobi and stuffed potatoes – to new takes on old themes – baked field mushrooms, chips and béarnaise; cheese croquettes and our own twist on cassoulet.

We have not called this chapter vegetarian. The idea is to celebrate main-course dishes made from seasonal fresh vegetables not necessarily to push the idea of excluding eating meat.

If you choose to buy organic that is your choice. What we want to encourage above all is using vegetables that are in brilliant condition and seasonal.

vegetables are very seasonal and our cooking styles should respect and reflect this.

'Cassoulet' with chilli and crème fraîche

225g flageolet beans, soaked overnight

2 onions

6 cloves

6 tablespoons olive oil

6 garlic cloves, finely chopped

2 red chillies, deseeded and finely chopped

1 teaspoon harissa

1 dessertspoon finely chopped rosemary

half dessertspoon finely chopped sage

1 tablespoon finely chopped parsley

1 cinnamon stick

1 teaspoon tomato purée

2 bay leaves

1 x 400g tin of chopped tomatoes

1 glass of white wine

2 parsnips, peeled

1 small red turnip, peeled

4 carrots, peeled

4 tablespoons crème fraîche

6 tablespoons breadcrumbs

2 tablespoons butter

Cook the beans in enough water to cover generously, along with a whole onion studded with the cloves. When the beans are tender, about 35-45 minutes, drain, reserving the liquid, and transfer to a shallow ovenproof dish. Preheat the oven to 220°C/gas mark 7.

Chop the other onion and gently sauté in 3 tablespoons of the olive oil for 10 minutes, without colouring. Add the garlic, chilli, harissa, herbs, cinnamon, tomato purée, bay leaves, chopped tomatoes and wine, and cook for a further 2 minutes. Roughly chop the root vegetables and lay in a baking tray. Toss with the remaining olive oil, season with salt and pepper and roast for 10 minutes in the preheated oven for 10 minutes, or until just coloured.

Combine everything in the ovenproof dish along with the crème fraîche and a seasoning of salt and pepper. Toss so everything is mixed well and pour in enough of the reserved bean liquid to come almost to the top of the mixture. Lower the oven temperature to 180°C/gas mark 4 and bake for $1^1/2$ hours. About 20 minutes before the end sprinkle over the breadcrumbs and dot with the butter. Serve with more crème fraîche.

Root vegetable cobbler

2 onions
bunch of parsley, leaves picked
4 peppercorns
1 vegetable stock cube, crumbled
3 carrots
2 parsnips
2 white turnips
1 small celeriac
2 sweet potatoes
4 tablespoons olive oil
half head of cauliflower
1 teaspoon finely chopped rosemary
1 teaspoon picked thyme leaves
1 bay leaf
half quantity of Shortcrust pastry (see page 109)

Preheat the oven to 220°C/gas mark 7. Roughly chop 1 of the onions and add to 850ml water in a pan, along with the parsley stalks, peppercorns and the vegetable stock cube. Bring to the boil, simmer for 15 minutes, strain this stock and reserve.Roughly chop all the vegetables, except the cauliflower, into 4cm cubes, toss in olive oil, scatter on to a roasting tray and roast in the preheated oven for 10 minutes, or until lightly charred. Reduce the oven to 180°C/gas mark 4.

Finely chop the remaining onion. In an ovenproof pan, gently sauté in the oil for 10-15 minutes. Add the stock, bring to the boil and add all the vegetables from the oven along with the cauliflower. Add the herbs (but not the parsley), season with salt and pepper and bring to the boil. Transfer to the oven, uncovered, and bake for 20 minutes.

Allow the mixture to cool slightly and add the chopped parsley. Roll the pastry into a circle large enough to overlap the tin. Lightly grease and flour the tin, lay the pastry inside and add the vegetable mixture. There should be a little liquid along with the vegetables, if you have too much (more than a tablespoon), drain it off. Fold the pastry loosely over the top and replace in the oven for 30-40 minutes.

Mushroom Wellington

serves 6-8

150g brown or Puy lentils, well rinsed

150g red split lentils

150g basmati rice

1kg field mushrooms, finely chopped

2 onions, finely chopped

3 garlic cloves, finely chopped

glass of red wine

1 teaspoon picked thyme

1 teaspoon picked oregano

1 tablespoon finely chopped parsley

100g feta, crumbled

2 sheets of puff pastry, rolled out into rectangles

1 egg, lightly beaten

Cook the lentils in plenty of boiling water for 10-12 minutes, or until tender. Cook the split peas and rice together in plenty of boiling salted water for 10-15 minutes, or until just tender. Drain.

Gently sauté the mushrooms and onions over a moderate heat for 10 minutes without allowing them to colour. Add the garlic, cook for a minute and then add the wine. Allow to boil away almost entirely (a few tablespoons of liquid is all that is required). Remove from the heat and stir in the lentils, rice and herbs. Season well with salt and pepper. Allow to cool.

Preheat the oven to 200°C/gas mark 6. Add the feta to the mixture and spoon on to the middle of a sheet of puff pastry. Brush the edges with the beaten egg and place the second sheet on top. Press firmly at the edges, score the top with a sharp knife to let the steam escape and then trim off the excess pastry leaving a sharp edge. This latter step is essential in getting the pastry to rise. Bake in the preheated oven for 30-40 minutes or until golden brown.

For the gravy   2 red onions, thinly sliced   4 tablespoons olive oil   1 teaspoon sugar   600ml cider
1 dessertspoon grainy mustard   1 teaspoon redcurrant jelly

Soften the onions in the olive oil for 15 minutes, allowing them to colour towards the end of cooking. Add the sugar and, when this darkens after a few minutes, pour in the cider. Boil down over a moderate heat for 20-30 minutes, or until reduced to a cupful. Stir in the mustard and the redcurrant jelly just before serving

Macaroni cheese

So traditional, this old classic is fast making a comeback on restaurant menus. The cheese is crucial to this dish, it needs to be a really good-quality, strong mature Cheddar. If you are tempted to use a milder cheese, the finished dish is likely to taste rather anaemic and will be a false economy as you will need a lot more cheese. Of the Irish cheeses, consider Doolin, a particularly strong and robust cheese.

75ml butter
75g flour
850ml milk
225g grated mature, extra-special, proper cheese (see above)
350g macaroni

Preheat the oven to 180°C/gas mark 4. Melt the butter, add the flour and cook, stirring constantly, over a low heat for 5 minutes. Add the milk and bring to the boil slowly, stirring all the time. Cook for 5 minutes, taking care it doesn't catch on the bottom, and set aside. Stir in three-quarters of the cheese, keeping the rest for the top.

Cook the pasta until just done. Combine with the sauce and pour into a buttered ovenproof dish, top with the remaining cheese and bake in the preheated oven for 20 minutes, or until golden and bubbling. This dish does not work if reheated.

Variations   Arrange tomato slices on top and, when it comes out of the oven, scatter over lots of roughly chopped basil.

Blanch a head of cauliflower, divided into florets, until just done, drain and refresh under cold water and combine with the pasta before adding to the mixture.

Gently stir 2 drained tins of tuna and 1 tin of drained sweetcorn through the mixture before adding to the ovenproof dish.

Baked endive with Cashel Blue and sage

4-5 heads of chicory
50g butter, plus more for greasing
bunch of sage, leaves picked
2 tablespoons roughly crumbled Cashel Blue
4 tablespoons breadcrumbs
2 tablespoons chopped parsley
200ml double cream
1 lemon, quartered

Preheat the oven to 180°C/gas mark 4. Trim the core from the stem end of the chicory and cut in half lengthways. Generously butter a shallow ovenproof dish and place the chicory, cut side down, in the dish. Season with salt and pepper.

Melt the butter in a frying pan and, when hot, drop in the sage leaves. They will sizzle and curl up. Remove from the heat and set aside.

Combine the cheese, breadcrumbs and parsley. Scatter the sautéed sage over the chicory, pour in the cream and scatter over the breadcrumb mixture. Drizzle over the sage butter and bake in the preheated oven for 30-40 minutes, or until brown and bubbling. Serve with lemon quarters.

Cheese croquettes

Croquettes may evoke images of hotel lunches in times past, but that doesn't make them any less delicious when well executed. They are popular throughout much of mainland Europe and with good reason. Perfect finger food for parties, they can also be served like the vegetarian version of fishcakes.

600ml milk
1 bay leaf
1 onion
1 blade of mace
1 carrot
bunch of parsley, finely chopped (stalks reserved)
150g butter
150g flour, plus more for dusting
225g extra-strong mature Cheddar
bunch of chives, snipped
2 teaspoons Dijon mustard
2 eggs, lightly beaten
fine dried breadcrumbs or matzo meal
oil, for frying

In a large pan, combine the milk with the bay leaf, onion, mace, carrot and parsley stalks. Bring to the boil and set aside to infuse for 20 minutes. Strain and return to the heat.

Combine the butter and flour in another saucepan and cook over a low heat, without allowing to colour, for 5 minutes. Spoon this mixture into the hot milk, whisking all the time. Doing it this way helps to avoid lumps and is easier to handle; which is rather crucial in this instance, because it is so thick.

Remove from the heat and sprinkle in the cheese, stirring all the time. The texture should be similar to smooth cement. Season generously with salt and pepper and stir in the chives and mustard. Spoon on to a plate, allow to cool and refrigerate for an hour.

Using your hands, roll the mixture into cylinders about 6cm long and 3cm wide. If the mixture is very sticky, dip your hands periodically into cold water. Roll each cylinder in seasoned flour, dip in the beaten egg and then roll in the breadcrumbs. Shallow- or deep-fry in hot oil for 4 minutes or until golden brown, then transfer to the preheated oven for 10 minutes, and serve when they are all ready. Serve with the relish on page 171, or treat yourself and buy a good tomato chutney.

Chilli bean bake

Heady with the flavour of spices, this bean dish is robust and packed with flavour. The chocolate acts to thicken everything at the end and is common in the cooking of Mexico.

100g dry kidney beans, soaked overnight
100g dry black-eyed beans, soaked overnight
1 onion, finely chopped
3 tablespoons olive oil
1 aubergine, trimmed and cut into 2cm chunks
1 teaspoon ground cumin
1 teaspoon ground coriander
1 red chilli, finely chopped
1 green chilli, finely chopped
5 garlic cloves, finely chopped
1 teaspoon harissa
1 red pepper, trimmed and diced
1 yellow pepper, trimmed and diced
100g mushrooms, quartered
1 tablespoon tomato purée
2 x 400g tins of tomatoes
half vegetable stock cube
1 glass of white wine
50g dark chocolate (55% cocoa solids)

In separate pans, in plenty of water, cook the beans for an hour or until tender, removing any scum that rises to the surface.

Preheat the oven to 180°C/gas mark 4. Gently sauté the onion in the olive oil for 10 minutes, without allowing it to colour. Add the diced aubergine, along with the spices and chillies. Cook, stirring, for 2 minutes. Add the garlic and harissa, peppers and mushrooms (if the mixture looks a little dry you may need a little more oil), and stir to coat them in the mixture. Add the tomato purée, tinned tomatoes, vegetable stock cube and enough water to cover the vegetables.

Transfer to the preheated oven and cook for 1 hour, uncovered. Remove from the oven and stir in the glass of white wine and chocolate. Serve with the relish on page 171 and Greek-style yoghurt or crème fraîche.

Aloo gobi

This is a classic, easily prepared Indian vegetarian dish that is excellent by itself, but also very good as an accompaniment to grilled meat and fish. It will also keep warm for an hour or so quite happily in a low oven, so it is useful for entertaining.

4 tablespoon vegetable oil

1 teaspoon mustard seeds

half teaspoon chilli flakes, or to taste

2 teaspoons cumin seeds

4 garlic cloves, finely chopped

2 onions, finely chopped

1 cauliflower, divided into florets

4 potatoes, peeled and roughly chopped

half teaspoon turmeric

half stock cube, crumbled

Heat the oil in a saucepan large enough to take all the ingredients. When hot, add the mustard seeds, chilli flakes and cumin seeds. As the spices start to pop, add the garlic and, as soon as it starts to colour, add the onions. Cook for 10 minutes without allowing to colour.

Add the cauliflower, potatoes and turmeric. Stir so everything is well coated, season with salt and pepper, turn the heat down. Pour in 300ml of water, add the stock cube and cover with the lid. Cook for 20 minutes, or until the potato and cauliflower are tender.

Serve with rice, yoghurt, chutney and naan bread, or as an accompaniment to grilled meat or fish.

Seeds

We use seeds extensively in the cafés. Apart from being delicious - an open packet of pumpkin seeds is an invitation to nibble - they provide both texture and colour to anything from salads to pastry, pâtés to soups.

When creating dishes, we are looking for both contrasting and complementary elements which, if successfully combined, are ultimately what leaves the person eating the dish feeling satisfied. For example, a salad that includes pumpkin seeds or sunflower seeds has a roundness that simply isn't the same if they are not included. With the exception of the onion seeds those listed below are used in our five-seed bread.

Onion seeds   Popular in both Indian and Middle Eastern cooking, onion seeds have a faintly peppery, spicy flavour that works well in salads. They work better with light vegetables rather than meat, the latter being rather too strong in flavour.

Sesame seeds   For something so small, this is a seed that gets about. Native to India, it turns up there, is used for its oil in Mexico along with the seed and in Japanese cooking gets regular billing. Then in the Middle East it turns up as tahini, while in the USA it is used in cakes and cookies. We generally use them in salads.

Poppy seeds   These come from the opium poppy, but with none of the associated side effects. The grey-blue seeds look very dramatic both in salads and in pastry and, while their flavour is slight, their size means they introduce a curious nuttiness.

Linseed   Tiny, piquant and curiously burning in the mouth, linseeds don't really taste of a great deal but they do give a feeling of depth to whatever they are added. We use them in salads and they are a part of the granola on page 62. They are highly nutritious and especially good for women.

Sunflower   These make the perfect nibbling snack as they are both healthy and nutritious, but don't carry quite the cholesterol of nuts. Their flavour is muted, but they provide a curious nuttiness to salads. You can buy the seeds still in their outer shell which are roasted with salt; each one is then opened individually, much like a pistachio.

Pumpkin   Much like sunflower seeds, pumpkin seeds add body but not a very strong flavour and again are used mostly in salads. They too are good for nibbling.

Clockwise from top left: Pumpkin seeds, onion seeds, sesame seeds, poppy seeds, linseeds and sunflower seeds

Baked field mushrooms, 'chips' and béarnaise

Field mushrooms, the big whoppers, have a flavour and texture not a million miles from steak. Cooked this way completes the transition, a veggie version of a classic steak dinner. This is not something we serve in the cafés, but an idea from one of our vegetarian chefs who said the only thing she really missed about a steak dinner was the chips and béarnaise. If you make up a large quantity of the reduction for the sauce as here, it will keep indefinitely in the fridge, which means you can whisk up a béarnaise in moments.

4 teaspoons butter
4 large field mushrooms (or 8 medium)
2 garlic cloves, finely chopped
for the chips
4 large floury potatoes
olive oil

Preheat the oven to 200°C/gas mark 6. Butter the top of each mushroom and then turn over and arrange on a tray. Put a teaspoon of butter into each mushroom and bake in the preheated oven for 20-30 minutes, or until wilted. Sprinkle over the garlic, cover the tray with foil and set aside. Turn the oven to its highest setting to cook the chips, far better to spread them out and use two trays rather than crowding them on to one. Swap the trays' positions over halfway through cooking.

For the chips, slice the potatoes, toss in olive oil, season with salt and pepper and roast in the oven for 20-25 minutes, or until golden. You need to turn them once or twice in the final 15 minutes of cooking, so they brown all over.

For the béarnaise   3 tablespoons white wine vinegar   1 packet of fresh tarragon, finely chopped
1 tablespoon finely chopped shallot   1 teaspoon cracked peppercorns   2 bay leaves   3 egg yolks   250g butter
1 packet of fresh chervil, finely chopped

Combine the vinegar with an equal quantity of water, a good handful of tarragon, the shallots, peppercorns and bay leaves in a stainless steel saucepan, bring to the boil and reduce until you have about a tablespoon of liquid. Remove the bay leaves and discard.

Melt the butter in a pan. Combine the egg yolks with the reduction and, over the lowest possible heat, cook briefly to thicken. Add the melted butter as you would do oil to egg yolks when making mayonnaise, stirring all the time until it thickens. Have a small jar of hot water to one side and, if it looks like over-thickening and splitting, add a little hot water. Remove from the heat, stir in the remaining herbs and check the seasoning. Serve with the chips and mushrooms.

Potato, parsnip, apple and Doolin gratin

The starch in the potatoes helps to make this a rich and creamy dish. It works well with grilled meats too. Doolin is a strong hard Irish cheese, similar to a strong Cheddar or Amsterdam, but with a slightly more waxy consistency. To skin hazelnuts, wrap in a tea towel and rub between your hands.

1 onion, thinly sliced

2 tablespoons butter, plus more for greasing

1 dessertspoon sugar

5 large potatoes, peeled and thinly sliced

2 parsnips, peeled and thinly sliced

2 Bramley apples, peeled, cored and thinly sliced

100g toasted hazelnuts, skinned and briefly blitzed in a food processor

100g Doolin, grated

600ml double cream

300ml full-fat milk

Preheat the oven to 180°C/gas mark 4. Gently sauté the onion in half the butter for 10 minutes. Add the sugar and allow to colour slightly for 5 minutes.

Lightly grease the bottom of a shallow ovenproof dish with a little butter. Layer up potatoes, onion, parsnip and apple. Scatter a little of the blitzed hazelnuts, a seasoning of salt and pepper and a sprinkling of the cheese as you go along. Finish with a layer of potatoes, this is important to keep a pale colour to the finished dish.

Combine the cream and milk, and pour into the dish. Finish the top with the remaining butter, hazelnuts and cheese. Bake in the preheated oven for 45 minutes.

Potatoes vary enormously through the year and from one variety to another. If you are tempted to reduce the cream content in this dish, bear in mind it can separate if the starch content in the potato is too low. One solution is to poach the potatoes and parsnips in the cream and milk first. Bring them to the boil and then turn the heat off and leave them to cool. When you are baking the dish, whichever route you go, keep an eye on it during the last 20 minutes; you may need to cover the top with foil to prevent it over-browning.

Keep an eye out for Carne potatoes in the summer months; these are the cream of the Wexford crop and can often be bought from roadside stalls. With butter and mint, there is nothing to beat them.

Stuffed potatoes

4 large rooster potatoes

1 courgette

half aubergine

1 red pepper

1 yellow pepper

6 tablespoons olive oil

1 tablespoon sun-dried tomato pesto

100g goat's cheese

2 tablespoons roughly chopped semi-sun-dried tomatoes

50g pitted black olives, roughly chopped

1 tablespoon shredded basil or thyme

Preheat the oven to 180°C/gas mark 4. Bake the potatoes, pricking them once or twice, for 45 minutes to 1 hour, or until cooked. Dice all the other vegetables, lightly toss in olive oil and season well with salt and pepper. Grill, tossing 2 or 3 times, for 10 minutes, or until lightly charred.

Cut the top off each potato and scoop out the inside. Mash this, adding the pesto, crumble in the goat's cheese and gently mix in the remaining ingredients except half the herbs. Season with salt and pepper and refill the potato skins. Return to the oven for 10 minutes to warm them through. If you have prepared them in advance, they will need 25 minutes. Sprinkle over some shredded basil or thyme and serve.

Variations   This is a great way to use leftovers: diced ham, finely chopped spring onions, mayonnaise and shredded mange tout; tuna, chives and sweetcorn.

In the café kitchens we generally use rooster potatoes during the autumn and winter months. Our experience is that white, or what are often referred to as 'baking', potatoes can have too high a water content at this time of year. As we move into the summer months, our menus change and we move into using new-season's potatoes. Some of the more interesting salad varieties include la ratte, pink fir apple and charlotte.

Spaghetti alla Genovese

If the idea of pairing pasta and potatoes seems a little odd, these two starches together are something of a revelation, the flavour of both enhanced by the liaison. We were first shown the dish by a visiting chef brought over to launch Anna Coleman's Delizie Italiane range, sold in all our shops.

serves 6
3 small new potatoes
225g young French beans
600g spaghetti or fettuccine
3 tablespoons pesto (see page 72)
freshly shaved Parmesan

Peel the potatoes and cut into 5mm slices. Blanch in boiling salted water for 5 minutes or until cooked, refresh in cold water and set aside. Trim the stem ends from the French beans, wash in cold water and cook in boiling salted water until tender but still al dente. Drain and set aside.

Cook the pasta in plenty of boiling salted water until al dente. Drain, reserving some of the cooking water. Toss the pasta with the potatoes, French beans and 2 tablespoons of the pesto. Taste and adjust with more pesto and cooking water. Serve immediately with Parmesan.

FISH

Simple is best with fish. Olive oil or butter and a squeeze of lemon juice will win out over a complicated sauce every time... provided, of course, your fish is fresh. Shopping is crucial. Be ruled by what you see. If it looks good and smells of the sea, buy it.

Whether you slap sea bass on hot coals and serve it up with a fiery salsa to excite, or roast cod and serve it with black pudding mash and hollandaise to soothe, you need to be dealing with the best.

Cultivate your fishmonger, he or she is a mine of information and useful too. Nobody really wants do the cleaning and scaling, but the fishmonger will do it.

If you go for prime fish every time, you'll pay for the privilege. Don't overlook the less expensive fish, like sea bream or mackerel, both of which like robust flavours to give of their best. And consider the comfort dishes like fish pie and fish cakes. These fly out the door whenever we have them on the menu.

Fish makes for fantastic eating, the perfect modern food. It marries enthusiastically with other flavours, is quick to prepare and cook, and makes for easy eating. Skip the shopping list and go and buy what's good, let your eyes do the talking.

Good fish smells sweet and salty, fresh and vibrant, healthy and invigorating – just like the sea

Farmed versus wild There is much development work being done that suggests the amount of farmed fish sold will increase substantially over the near future. Already a lot of the sea bass and sea bream sold is farmed, halibut is being trialed, as is cod. There is nothing inherently wrong with farmed fish, but there is a world of difference between good and bad farmed fish. For the consumer the real concern is the lack of proper standards and in the short term you are forced to rely on the honesty of your fishmonger. A lot of the sea bass sold is now farmed in the Mediterranean. Unlike salmon however, most fishmongers fail to point this out. If all the fish is the same size, question closely. Nature is not known for its consistency, wild sea bass tend to come in a range of sizes. When buying salmon, go for wild if at all possible, organic farmed is the next best thing.

Buying cooked shellfish (lobsters and crabs particularly) Most fishmongers cook large batches, say 20 crabs, so the smaller ones inevitably end up overcooked. How much salt did he use? And what was the quality of the seafood before it was cooked? Unless you know your fishmonger very well, it is generally better to cook shellfish yourself.

What to look for when you buy Bright eyes, shiny, bright, taut skin. Slime on fish is good. Good fish don't smell of anything other than the sea, sweet and salty. Fish are often filleted as they deteriorate, it's harder to tell when the head has gone. If possible always get a fish filleted in front of you from a whole fish.

How much to buy? Allow about 180g to 200g for a main course of pure fish. If you are buying a whole fish, you will lose about half its weight in bones and skin.

Storing fish Fish should be stored at zero degrees centigrade. A domestic fridge commonly operates at around 5 degrees. If you have to store fish, re-wrap in clingfilm when you get home and keep in the coldest part, which is often the shelf closest to the freezer box.

Smoked fish Smoked haddock comes in two forms, vibrantly yellow, and in a gentle, washed out pink version. The latter has been naturally smoked, the former may have been smoked, but it has also been treated with a dye to colour it. Which is better? The naturally smoked version is the more pure of the two.

Some ingredients that go well with fish Pastis (brands like Pernod and Ricard), saffron, paprika, fennel (seeds as well as the vegetable), dry vermouth, capers, soy sauce, really really good olive oil, lemon, salted black beans.

Grilled sea bass, spinach and chickpea pilaf and raita

half cucumber, grated

1 onion, finely chopped

3 tablespoons vegetable oil

half teaspoon black mustard seeds

1 teaspoon cumin seeds

4 cloves

4 cardamom pods

1 teaspoon turmeric

half teaspoon fennel seeds

6cm piece of cinnamon

1 mug of basmati rice

1 x 400g tin of chickpeas, drained and rinsed

800g spinach, washed and roughly chopped

100ml plain yoghurt

1 garlic clove, finely chopped and mashed with a little salt

4 fillets of sea bass

1 lemon, quartered

Add a teaspoon of salt to the cucumber, toss, place in a sieve and set aside. Gently sauté the onion in the oil for 10 minutes, or until soft but not browned. Add the mustard and cumin seeds, cloves, cardamom pods, turmeric, fennel seeds and cinnamon, and cook for a further 2 minutes or until the spices lose their raw aroma.

Add the rice and chickpeas, stirring so everything is well coated in the oil. Stir in enough water to cover by 1cm, season with salt and pepper and put on the lid with a sheet of greaseproof paper between it and the pan to improve the seal. Cook for 10 minutes, remove from the heat and set aside without disturbing the lid. Blanch the spinach in boiling salted water for 2 minutes or until just tender, drain and refresh in cold water. Drain again and gently squeeze out as much liquid as possible. Roughly chop and stir into the rice and chickpeas. This is the pilaf.

Rinse the cucumber under plenty of running water and squeeze as much moisture from it as possible. Combine with the yoghurt and garlic and set aside. This is the raita.

Preheat the grill and cook the sea bass for 3 minutes, skin side down. Turn over and continue grilling for a further 4 minutes, or until cooked. Serve the sea bass on top of the pilaf with the raita and a lemon quarter.

Chargrilled sea bream, courgette and avocado salsa

1 red pepper
4 courgettes
7-8 tablespoons olive oil
bunch of fresh oregano
1 ripe avocado
half bunch of mint
half bunch of parsley
dash of balsamic vinegar
dash of Tabasco sauce (optional)
4 sea bream, each about 350g, cleaned but left whole with scales intact

Chargrill the red pepper until blackened all over, wrap in cling film and set aside.

Cut the courgettes into strips about 5mm wide and chargrill until just coloured. Transfer to a bowl as they are done, seasoning with salt and pepper and tossing with olive oil and a sprig or two of oregano as you go.

When the red pepper is cool, peel, deseed and dice. Halve and stone the avocado. To remove the stone, hold the half avocado with the stone in your hand, protected with a tea towel. Bring the knife down sharply on the stone and twist. Dice (about 5mm), discarding the skin. Finely chop the mint and parsley. Combine the red pepper, avocado, mint and parsley with 4-5 tablespoons of olive oil, a dash of balsamic vinegar and a generous dash of Tabasco, or not, depending on your liking for chilli.

Cut 2 slashes in each side of each fish, season well inside and out with coarse sea salt and pepper and barbecue for about 5 minutes on each side.

Serve with the courgettes and a generous dollop of the salsa.

Steamed mackerel, black bean sauce and glass noodles
Glass noodles cook amazingly quickly and have a deliciously smooth texture.

2 dessertspoons light soy sauce

2 tablespoons vegetable oil

1 tablespoon finely chopped ginger

2 tablespoons salted black beans, rinsed and roughly chopped

4 garlic cloves, finely chopped

2 tablespoons dry sherry

2 large mackerel, filleted

1 packet (250g) of glass noodles

1 tablespoon sesame oil

2 tablespoons chopped spring onions

handful of fresh coriander, roughly chopped

1 lemon, quartered

Combine the soy sauce, vegetable oil, ginger, black beans, garlic and sherry. Make a tray out of foil and pour the mixture into it. Either use a roasting tray, as in the picture on page 162, or a steaming basket, which will alter the shape and size of the foil tray. Lay the mackerel fillets, skin side up, in the mixture and set aside for at least 30 minutes, an hour is better.

Pour boiling water into the roasting tray or steamer and place over a moderate heat. Cover with a lid or more foil and cook for 8 minutes, or until the mackerel is cooked.

Pour boiling water over the glass noodles and leave to soften for 2 minutes, drain and toss with the sesame oil.

Serve the mackerel with the noodles, a sprinkling of spring onions and coriander, and a lemon wedge.

Being an oily fish, mackerel spoils quickly, so ensure you buy really fresh specimens. Look for bright eyes, tight skin and a sweet smell of the sea.

Previous page: Steamed mackerel, black bean sauce and glass noodles

Spiced swordfish steaks

2 tablespoons cumin seeds
4 garlic cloves, finely chopped
2 tablespoons paprika
pinch of cayenne pepper or finely chopped chilli
bunch of parsley, picked over
bunch of coriander, picked over
4 tablespoons white wine vinegar
juice of 1 lemon
generous dash of good olive oil
4 swordfish steaks

Blitz all the ingredients except the fish in a food processor with enough olive oil to form a thick sauce. Gently heat in a small saucepan without boiling and set aside. Preheat a hot grill. Brush the swordfish lightly with more olive oil and season with salt and pepper. Grill for 2-3 minutes on each side and serve with the spice mixture.

Halibut, basil crème fraîche, pea and mint purée

4 halibut steaks, each weighing about 150g
4 tablespoons olive oil
juice of 1 lemon
200g frozen peas
50g butter
large bunch of mint, finely chopped
large bunch of basil, picked and finely shredded
150g crème fraîche

Combine the fish with the olive oil, a seasoning of salt and pepper and the lemon juice. Toss gently and set aside for an hour. Preheat the oven to 220°C/gas mark 7. Roast the halibut for 10 minutes, or until cooked. Allow to rest for 5 minutes. Cook the peas with the butter in a covered pan until tender but still vibrantly green, about 3 minutes. Purée or push through a mouli-légume. Finely chop the mint and mix in with the peas. Combine the basil and crème fraîche. Serve the halibut with the pea purée and a spoonful of the basil crème fraîche on top.

Fishcakes with wilted spinach and parsley sauce

makes 4 large or 8 small fishcakes

450g floury potatoes

100g butter

1 large onion, finely chopped

225g smoked haddock

225g fresh cod

225g salmon

1 bay leaf

1 tablespoon each chopped dill and chives

2 tablespoons finely chopped flat leaf parsley

grated zest of 3 lemons

6 tablespoons dried breadcrumbs

3 tablespoons plain flour

2 eggs, lightly beaten

vegetable oil, for frying

for the parsley sauce

100g butter   75g plain white flour   about 600ml milk   big bunch of flat-leaf parsley, finely chopped

for the wilted spinach

2 tablespoons vegetable oil   1kg spinach

Cook the potatoes, drain and mash with 50g of the butter and season. with salt and pepper. Sauté the onion in the remaining 50g of butter for 10 minutes, without colouring. Place the fish in cold salted water with the bay leaf, bring to the boil and turn off. Remove the fish, flake and combine with the potato, onion, dill, chives, half the parsley, and the zest of 2 of the lemons. Check the seasoning and mould into 4 large or 8 small cakes.

Combine the breadcrumbs with the remaining lemon zest and parsley. Dip each fishcake, first in the flour, then in the egg and then in the breadcrumbs. Heat the vegetable oil and fry the fishcakes over a moderate heat for 3-4 minutes on each side, or until golden brown. Transfer to a preheated oven, 200°C/gas mark 6 for 10 minutes. Meanwhile, make the parsley sauce: melt the butter and stir in the flour. Cook for 2 minutes, stirring all the time, without allowing to colour. Stir in the milk and whisk well to get rid of any lumps. Heat until bubbling and the consistency of double cream (you may need a little more milk). Chop the parsley, stalks and all, and add to the sauce. Check for seasoning and serve.

To make the wilted spinach: heat a wok or large frying pan and, when hot, add the oil. As soon as it starts smoking, add the spinach, toss well so it wilts and remove 2 minutes later.

Pastrami salmon

Pastrami is originally spiced smoked beef and this recipe takes the principle but applies it to salmon instead. These amounts will feed 4 as a main course or 8 as a starter.

1kg salmon, trimmed (middle section, skin on, bone removed)
olive oil, for brushing
1 tablespoon onion seeds, dry roasted in a hot frying pan
bunch of chervil, picked

for the marinade
1 tablespoon salt
1 tablespoon light brown sugar
6 juniper berries, crushed
1 teaspoon smoked pimenton
2 garlic cloves, smashed and chopped
half onion, grated
1 tablespoon Dijon mustard
2 tablespoons finely chopped parsley
1 teaspoon crushed fennel seeds
half teaspoon freshly ground black pepper
small glass of vodka

Combine all the ingredients for the marinade and gently rub into the flesh side of the fish. Wrap tightly in cling film and place on a plate, skin side up, in the fridge for 24 hours.

Preheat the oven as high as it will go. Gently rub the marinade off with kitchen paper. Cut the fish into 4 fillets. Brush lightly with olive oil and sear in a hot heavy-based frying pan - it needs to be as hot as possible. Slide the fish in, skin side down, and do not touch for at least 3 minutes. Turn over and transfer to the hot oven.

The salmon can be served rare, as in raw in the middle, or cooked through, according to taste. For rare, roast for 4-5 minutes, for cooked about 8 minutes. Remove and allow to rest for 5 minutes.

With a very sharp knife, cut each fillet into 4 slices. Serve with the rémoulade (see page 94) with the onion seeds scattered through it and lots of chopped chervil.

Salmon, green peppercorns and capers

4 salmon fillets, each weighing about 180g

2 tablespoons olive oil, plus more for drizzling

4 handfuls of spinach, well rinsed

2 garlic cloves, finely chopped

3cm piece of ginger, peeled and grated

1 glass of white wine

2 tablespoons capers, well rinsed

2 tablespoons green peppercorns in brine, well rinsed

1 lemon, quartered

Lightly coat the salmon in olive oil, season well with salt and pepper. Heat a frying pan and, when it is almost smoking, add the salmon. Cook for 3 minutes, turn over and cook for the same time on the other side. Lower the heat, cover the pan with foil and cook for a further 3-4 minutes, or until the fish is cooked. Remove and keep warm.

Add the spinach to the pan and toss in the hot juices until it just starts to wilt. Add the garlic and ginger, toss in the hot pan briefly, remove and keep warm.

Add the wine to the hot pan, along with the capers and peppercorns, and boil to reduce the liquid by half. Season with salt and pepper.

Place the salmon on top of the wilted spinach, spoon over the pan juices along with the capers and green peppercorns, and serve with a lemon quarter and a generous drizzle of olive oil.

Seared tuna with tomato, avocado and caper relish

4 tuna steaks, each weighing about 180g

olive oil, for brushing

1 lemon, quartered, to serve

for the tomato, avocado and caper relish

1 teaspoon black mustard seeds

juice of $^1/_2$ lemon

6 plum tomatoes

1 tablespoon well rinsed capers

1 avocado, diced

1 tablespoon finely chopped coriander

1 red chilli, finely chopped

about 4 tablespoons olive oil

First make the relish: soak the mustard seeds in the lemon juice. Plunge the tomatoes into boiling water for 30 seconds and remove. Cut into quarters and remove the skins and the seeds, which should be discarded. Combine the quartered tomatoes with the black mustard seeds and lemon juice, the capers, avocado, coriander and chilli. Add enough olive oil to form a loose sauce.

Lightly brush the tuna with olive oil and season with salt and pepper. Heat a ridged griddle pan and, when really hot, cook for 2 minutes on each side. Tuna is far better when rare in the centre, but cook for longer if this is not to your taste.

Serve with the relish and a lemon quarter on each plate.

Grilled cod, black pudding mash and hollandaise

800g floury potatoes (e.g. Kerr's pinks)

200g black pudding

1 tablespoon butter

800g cod fillet cut into 4 or 8 pieces

2 tablespoons olive oil

300ml full-fat milk

1 bay leaf

8 peppercorns

for the hollandaise

3 tablespoons white wine vinegar   1 slice of onion   1 blade of mace   8 peppercorns   3 egg yolks

200g unsalted butter, cubed   juice of 1 lemon

First make the hollandaise: combine the white wine vinegar with the onion, mace and peppercorns, add 3 tablespoons of water and simmer until reduced to 1 tablespoon of liquid. Strain and squeeze into a oven-proof glass bowl. Add the egg yolks and place the bowl over a pan of barely simmering water. Whisk in the butter a cube at a time and when it is all added, check the seasoning and add lemon juice to taste. Remove from the heat but leave over the hot water and set aside, stirring occasionally, it will be quite happy for half an hour.

Boil the potatoes in their skins until cooked, 15-20 minutes. Remove the skins - it's hot work but has to be done - and mash. Gently fry the black pudding in the butter and tip into the mashed potato. Heat the milk with the bay leaf and peppercorns, strain and whisk into the potato.

Lightly oil the cod, season with salt and pepper and grill, skin side down for 2 minutes. Turn skin side up and grill for a further 5 minutes or until golden brown and cooked through.
Serve the fish on top of the mash, with a generous quantity of hollandaise.

Roast cod, haricot beans and paprika

Paprika comes in two forms, hot and sweet. Look for Spanish or Hungarian brands rather than international ones for flavour. Use the hot version when you want a mild chilli flavour. The sweet one is more often used in delicate dishes.

200g haricot beans, soaked overnight, drained and well rinsed
generous pinch of saffron strands
4 tablespoons hot water
4 tablespoons olive oil
1 onion, finely chopped
2 garlic cloves, finely chopped
1 tablespoon finely chopped flat-leaf parsley
grated zest of 1 lemon, plus 1 lemon to serve
half teaspoon sweet paprika
4 firm thick fillets of cod

Cover the beans with plenty of cold water and bring to the boil, simmer for 45 minutes to 1 hour and drain. Alternatively use two 400g tins, well rinsed and drained.

Soak the saffron strands in the hot water. Heat the olive oil and gently sauté the onion for 10-15 minutes without allowing to colour. Add the beans, garlic, parsley, lemon zest and paprika, and toss well in the oil. Add barely enough water to cover, cook gently for further 20 minutes and remove from the heat.

Preheat the oven to as high as it will go. Lightly oil the cod, season well with salt and pepper and place on a roasting tray, skin side down. Spoon over the saffron strands and liquid and roast in the oven for 8-10 minutes, or until cooked - the flesh should just flake when eased with a sharp knife.

Serve the cod on top of the beans, along with the lemon quarters.

Mussels, monkfish, sweet potato and saffron stew

1kg mussels, well washed and rinsed

150ml white wine

4 tablespoons olive oil

1 onion, chopped

2 garlic cloves, chopped

4 sweet potatoes, peeled and roughly chopped

200ml light fish or chicken stock

grated zest and juice of 1 lemon

generous pinch of saffron strands

1 bay leaf

500g monkfish, cut into 3cm chunks

Place the mussels in a saucepan over a high heat (rejecting any that fail to close when handled or tapped sharply on a hard surface), pour in the wine, cover and steam until they just open, 5 minutes or so. Allow to cool and reserve the juices. Remove the shells from two-thirds of the mussels, leaving the remaining third intact (discard any that didn't open). Strain the liquor to remove any grit.

Heat the olive oil and gently soften the onion for 10 minutes without colouring. Add the garlic, sweet potatoes and some seasoning. Cook, stirring continuously, for a further 2 minutes and then add the chicken stock and the zest and juice from the lemon. Bring to the boil, add the reserved mussel liquor, saffron strands, bay leaf, check the seasoning and simmer for 20-30 minutes, or until the sweet potato is tender.

About 10 minutes from the end, add the monkfish. When the monk-fish is cooked add the mussels and heat through for a further two minutes. Check seasoning and serve.

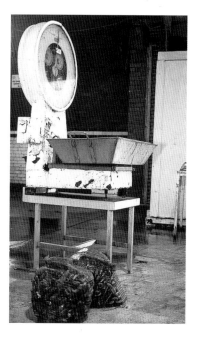

Mussels: Sublime, succulent, sweet, iodine-laced and surprisingly inexpensive, these blue-black shellfish are versatile and offer stunning eating. Whether stuffed with garlic-rich breadcrumbs heady with butter and flashed under the grill, or fashioned into a cream- and wine-rich soup, they taste so much of the sea – fresh, sweet and salty.

MEAT

While warm summer days are perfect for spiced lamb burgers – barbecued, perhaps, or chicken wrapped in Parma ham and stuffed with ricotta - the chill winds of autumn and winter are more suited to the likes of shepherd's pie or old-fashioned beef stew. Our weather is always in a state of change and this chapter aims to offer a range of dishes to suit all occasions.

This chapter also aims to use both the prime cuts and those that are a little less expensive - chicken thighs in the Thai green curry for example, or sausages with the lentils and chilli relish.

For a variety of different reasons the quality of meat sold is infinitely better than used to be the case, but care is still required. In beef, for example, lean meat with a rosy hue may look pleasant, but rarely translates into good eating; beef should be dark in colour and have a good marbling of fat running through it. Look out, too, for small-scale local producers. In pork we have also moved away from the idea of leanness being all-important and come to recognize the superior eating in some of the older breeds.

It may seem odd, but we would advocate eating less meat while at the same time focusing on shopping well for what you do buy.

A good butcher is well worth cultivating. They are often a mine of information on alternative cuts and how to obtain the best value

Old-fashioned beef stew

This beef stew was first made for Leylie's daughter Harley. The idea was to develop something simple to prepare after work, which was homely and comforting. This recipe serves 6-8, but it does freeze well and taste even better the following day.

1 onion, finely chopped
8 tablespoons olive oil
1kg round or chuck steak, about 3cm thick, cut into 3cm dice
2 tablespoons seasoned flour
6 carrots, cut into 3cm rounds
half head of celery, finely chopped
100g button mushrooms
1 x 400g tin of tomatoes
2 tablespoons Godalls browning or Worcestershire sauce

Preheat the oven to 180°C/gas mark 4. In an ovenproof casserole, gently sauté the onion in half the olive oil for 10 minutes without allowing it to colour. Toss the meat in the seasoned flour and brown in the remaining olive oil in a separate pan in batches.

Add the meat to the onions, along with the carrots, celery, mushrooms, tomatoes and browning. Season with salt and pepper and add just enough water to cover, cover with the lid and transfer to the preheated oven for 1 hour, or until cooked. Serve with mashed potatoes.

Parma-wrapped fillet of lamb with Savoy cabbage

1 onion, finely chopped

50g bacon lardons

1 tablespoon butter

5 garlic cloves, finely chopped

1 Savoy cabbage, trimmed and finely shredded

2 tablespoons picked fresh thyme

400ml double cream

about 16 large spinach leaves

2 boned fillets of lamb

2 tablespoons olive oil

8-12 slices of Parma ham

Preheat the oven to 200°C/gas mark 6. Gently sauté the onion and bacon in the butter for 10 minutes without colouring. Add the garlic, cook for a further 3 minutes, stirring, then add the cabbage, thyme and cream. Cover and cook gently over a low heat, stirring frequently for 10 minutes. Remove the cabbage, increase the heat and reduce the liquid by two-thirds, stirring occasionally. Set aside. Blanch the spinach leaves and refresh in iced water. Sear the lamb in a hot pan with the oil for a scant minute each side. Allow to cool.

Form a rectangle with the Parma ham, laying the slices alongside each other so they just overlap. Lay the spinach leaves on top and then the lamb fillet. Spoon 3 tablespoons of the cabbage mixture on top of each fillet and roll each parcel up. Roast in the preheated oven for 15-20 minutes depending on how you like your lamb. Remove and allow to rest for at least 5 minutes, preferably 10. Slice with a very sharp knife and serve with the remaining cabbage and the cream, as well as the juices left in the roasting tin.

Tagine of lamb with root vegetable couscous

This is a Moroccan dish which gets its name from the utensil in which it is traditionally cooked. Pyramidal in shape, it is generally earthenware and traditionally went on an open fire. They make for a dramatic entrance on any table, but a good-quality casserole works just as well. This makes more than you need for four, but it does freeze well and certainly tastes better if you make it a day or two ahead.

serves 6-8

1 teaspoon ground cumin

1 teaspoon ground coriander

quarter teaspoon ground turmeric

2 tablespoons well-seasoned flour

1kg leg of lamb, diced

olive oil

1 onion, diced

3 garlic cloves, finely chopped

1 red chilli

6cm piece of fresh ginger, peeled and grated

bunch of fresh coriander, leaves picked and roughly chopped, stalks finely chopped

1 dessertspoon treacle

handful of good-quality sultanas

half 400g tin of tomatoes

50g flaked almonds

250g couscous

400g finely diced carrot, parsnip and turnip

Preheat the oven to 180°C/gas mark 4. Mix all the dry spices together with a teaspoon of ground black pepper and the seasoned flour. Toss the meat in this mixture and brown in batches in the oil so it is nicely browned.

Gently sauté the onion in 4 tablespoons of the oil in an ovenproof casserole for 10 minutes or until softened. Add the garlic, chilli and ginger and coriander stalks, toss so they are well coated in the oil and add in the lamb. Barely cover with water and add the treacle, sultanas and tomatoes. Bring to the boil. Transfer to the preheated oven and bake for 1 hour or until cooked. Check halfway through cooking; you may need to add a little more water. Toast the flaked almonds in the top of the oven until golden. Cook the couscous according to the instructions on the packet. Blanch the root vegetables in boiling salted water until just tender, drain and combine with cooked couscous. Scatter the almonds over the tagine and serve with the couscous.

Herbs

If we have a secret weapon at Avoca, it is probably herbs. We use lots of them in pretty much every savoury thing we cook. They add depth of flavour, complexity and colour to everything from salads to stews, quiches to pâtés.

Buying supermarket herbs is a bit soul-destroying. They cost a fortune and come in amounts so small you are discouraged from using them in sufficient quantities. The simple answer is to grow your own, a task not difficult and not impossible, even for those who might have to rely on a window box.

Rosemary   Associated with lamb, this herb has many other uses and, finely chopped, is particularly good with sautéed potatoes. Use also in stews (beef as well as lamb) and with veal, sausages and pork.

Coriander   You can use every part of the coriander plant from the delicate leaves right through to the stem, root and seed. In general the leaves are added towards the end of cooking as they tend to collapse with heat and lose their pungency. Both the stem and root, however, can be finely chopped and introduced earlier, as they stand up to heat.

Sage   With its smoky, meaty flavour, sage deserves wider use than it generally gets. A classic with calf's liver, it is also useful in vegetarian dishes to add weight. Sage butter is an easy and effective way to cheer up a grilled chop or piece of fish, and if you are feeling adventurous consider dipping leaves in milk and then flour and deep-frying them. They make a better snack than crisps.

Dill   Generally associated with northern Europe and fish dishes in particular, dill also works well with chicken and creamy dishes, as well as salads, the feathery fronds imparting a gentle aniseed flavour.

Tarragon   A classic with chicken, a must in béarnaise, tarragon is also delicious in green salads and adds a stylish flourish if stirred into many soups and stews just before serving.

Basil   The classic herb with tomatoes, basil is also good in salads - indeed most dishes involving tomatoes benefit from fresh basil leaves. Their flavour disappears when cooked, so add at the last minute.

Thyme   As good with beef as with pork, lamb, poultry and game, thyme is one of the herbs we use most frequently and, unusually, generally at the beginning of cooking.

Oregano   One of the few herbs that really is excellent dried, oregano has a wide range of uses and finds its way into stews and casseroles as much as meat roasts and with fish - although a light touch is required with fish; it is quite powerful.

From top, left to right: coriander, rosemary, sage, tarragon, basil, dill, thyme, oregano

Chicken, mushroom and asparagus lasagne

4 chicken breasts
1 onion
1 carrot
2 celery sticks
bunch of parsley, leaves picked
1 bay leaf
bunch of asparagus, trimmed and cut into 4cm pieces, keeping 3 stalks whole
75g butter
110g sliced mushrooms
75g flour
300ml double cream
1 teaspoon fresh thyme
1 teaspoon fresh tarragon
1 packet of no-cook lasagne sheets
about 50g grated Parmesan

Poach the chicken breasts in 400ml of water with the onion, carrot, celery, parsley stalks and bay leaf for 25 minutes or until cooked. Remove the chicken and strain what is now a rather delicious stock.

Preheat the oven to 180°C/gas mark 4. Blanch all the asparagus for 4 minutes in the stock, remove with a slotted spoon and refresh under cold water. Reserve the stock for the sauce.

In a separate pan, melt the butter, add the mushrooms, season well and cook for 5 minutes or until the juices run. Remove the mushrooms, add the flour to the liquid and cook for 5 minutes on a low heat, stirring all the time. This stage is important to cook the floury taste out and keep as much of the mushroom flavour in as possible. Gradually add the reserved chicken stock and then the cream, whisking continuously to ensure there are no lumps.

Dice the chicken breasts quite small, about 2cm, and combine with the chopped asparagus, sliced mushrooms, herbs and three-quarters of the sauce.

Assemble the lasagne in the normal way by putting alternating layers of the chicken mixture and pasta in a large deep rectangular ovenproof dish, finishing off with a layer of pasta. Pour over the reserved sauce, sprinkle over vast quantities of Parmesan and bake in the preheated oven for 30-40 minutes, or until golden brown and bubbling. About 5 minutes before the end, place the remaining asparagus spears on top and heat through in the oven.

O'NEILL'S

STOKES
CORK

M.J. O'NEILL 2

While there is no point in using your best claret to cook with refrain from going for the cheapest you can find, if you aren't prepared to drink it you shouldn't be cooking with it

WINES

SPIRITS

Chicken, garlic, red wine and bay leaves

For such a short list of ingredients, this dish is decidedly full flavoured. The crucial item is the chicken – if it is good, then this dish is sensational. The wine, too, is important, it should be something weighty like good Rioja

serves 6

2 free-range chickens, jointed into 8 and scored

8-10 tablespoons olive oil

12 bay leaves

3 whole heads of garlic, broken into cloves, skins left on

$3/4$ bottle of red wine, such as Rioja

Heat the olive oil in a heavy-bottomed shallow pan, place the chicken in it, skin side down, and season well. Cook on a high heat for 10-15 minutes, turning once until golden brown on both sides. Add the bay leaves, garlic cloves and red wine, and cook for a further 20-25 minutes, uncovered, turning occasionally until the wine has reduced by a third. Serve with crusty bread to soak up the juices.

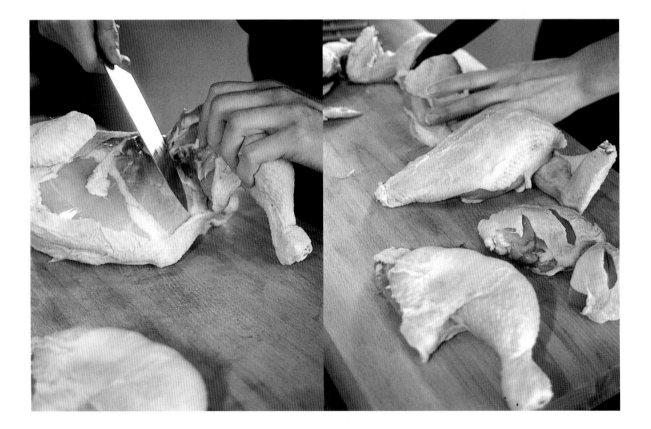

Chicken, veal and spinach cannelloni

300ml double cream
600ml full-fat milk
2 onions, peeled
1 carrot
blade of mace
half teaspoon freshly grated nutmeg
150g butter
250g chicken or turkey, minced
250g cushion of veal, minced
175g ricotta
225g Parmesan, finely grated
1 dessertspoon each roughly chopped thyme, sage, tarragon and basil
2 generous handfuls of baby spinach, chopped
75g flour
16 cannelloni tubes

Preheat the oven to 180°C/gas mark 4. Combine the cream and milk with one of the onions, the carrot, mace and nutmeg. Bring to the boil and set aside to infuse. Very finely chop the remaining onion and gently sauté in 50g of the butter for 10-15 minutes, or until soft.

Put the cooked chopped onion in a bowl with the chicken and veal, the ricotta, half the Parmesan, the herbs and spinach and season well with salt and pepper. A common mistake is to under-season at this point. We would always fry a teaspoon of the mixture to check. To do this, flatten the mixture and sauté for 2 minutes on each side. Adjust seasoning in the main mixture accordingly.

Add the remaining butter to the same pan that you used to cook the onion, followed by the flour, and cook over a gentle heat for 5 minutes. Strain the infused milk into this mixture and continue cooking, stirring all the time, until thick. Season with salt and pepper.

If you have a piping bag, the next job is easy; if you insist on using a teaspoon, you are going to have a long and messy task ahead of you. Spoon a little of the sauce over the bottom of a rectangular shallow ovenproof dish. Stuff each cannelloni with the mixture and lay on top of the sauce. Pour over the remaining sauce, making sure some sinks down between the tubes; if the pasta is left together it will get dry and tough.

Sprinkle over the remaining Parmesan and bake in the preheated oven for 40 minutes, or until brown and bubbling.

Green chicken curry

The red and green in Thai curries comes from the colour of the chilli used, one can be just as hot as the other. The paste will keep for a few days if refrigerated and covered with a layer of vegetable oil. It also freezes well. Most Asian stores sell red and green curry paste, which are good store-cupboard standbys to have for when you are in a rush. Authentic Thai food is incredibly refreshing and a sensible hand with coconut milk is essential; too much and the dish may taste rich, but this can soon become sickly.

2 tablespoons vegetable oil

1 garlic clove, finely chopped

125ml coconut cream

2 tablespoons fish sauce (nam pla)

1 tablespoon sugar

8 chicken thighs, chopped

125ml chicken stock

2 kaffir lime leaves, chopped

1 tablespoon sliced bamboo shoot

1 tablespoon roughly chopped coriander

for the green curry paste

10 green chillies, chopped   1 teaspoon ground coriander seeds $^1/_2$ teaspoon ground cumin
1 tablespoon finely chopped lemon grass $^1/_2$ teaspoon ground white pepper
2 tablespoons finely chopped shallots   4 garlic cloves, finely chopped   4 kaffir lime leaves, thinly sliced
(fresh if possible, otherwise dried)   3 cm piece of galangal, peeled and finely chopped   2 teaspoons fish sauce
large bunch of coriander, roots and all, chopped   1 teaspoon salt

First make the green curry paste: combine all the ingredients in a mortar and crush to a paste with the pestle. These quantities will give you about 3 tablespoons.

Heat the oil and, when hot, add the garlic and fry until golden brown. Add 2 tablespoons of the curry paste, stir-fry for a few seconds and then add the coconut cream. Stir until it curdles and thickens in the oil. Add the fish sauce, sugar and chicken, stir and cook for 5 minutes. Add the stock, bring to the boil, lower the heat and simmer until the meat is cooked through, a minute or two. Add the lime leaves, bamboo shoots and coriander leaves, and pour into a serving dish.

Rice to serve with Thai curries: Jasmine, Thai and basmati rice all go well with Thai curries.

Parma-wrapped chicken breasts with ricotta stuffing

This makes an impressive dish for entertaining and has the added advantage that much of the preparation can be done in advance. You can stuff and wrap the breasts and then store them in the fridge for the next day.

1 small tub of ricotta
1 tablespoon crème fraîche
2 handfuls of baby spinach, roughly chopped
50g chopped dried apricots
half bunch of spring onions, chopped
1 teaspoon chopped fresh tarragon
freshly grated nutmeg
2 tablespoons grated Parmesan
4 corn-fed chicken breasts
8 thin slices of Parma ham
glass of chicken stock (optional)

Preheat the oven to 180°C/gas mark 4. Combine the ricotta, crème fraîche, spinach, apricots, spring onions, tarragon, nutmeg and Parmesan, and season well with salt and pepper.

Make a pocket in each chicken breast and fill with the ricotta mixture. Wrap each breast in 2 slices of Parma ham. Put a glass of chicken stock or water in a casserole dish, lay the chicken breasts in it, cover and cook for 25 minutes in the preheated oven. Remove the cover and carry on cooking for 10 minutes, or until cooked.

Serve with mash (see page 200) and braised red cabbage below.

Braised red cabbage   1 small red cabbage   3 tablespoons white wine vinegar   2 tablespoons sugar
4 apples, peeled, cored and grated   1 teaspoon ground cumin   2 teaspoons ground coriander   4 whole cloves
1 cinnamon stick   100g butter

Preheat the oven to 170°C/gas mark 3. Remove the outer leaves from the cabbage, quarter it, remove the core and shred finely. In a bowl, combine with all the rest of the ingredients and pack into a heavy casserole. Bake in the preheated oven for 2 hours, stirring occasionally to prevent anything catching.

Duck shepherd's pie

serves 6

6 duck legs and 2 breasts, preferably male

3 glasses of red wine

1 teaspoon rosemary

1 teaspoon marjoram

1 tablespoon thyme

1 tablespoon parsley

1 onion, finely chopped

2 garlic cloves

2 tablespoons Worcestershire sauce

2 x 400g tins of tomatoes

2 large carrots, diced

2 parsnips, diced

a little vegetable or chicken stock

1 tablespoon redcurrant jelly

for the mash topping

6 large floury potatoes, peeled and chopped   1 small celeriac, peeled and chopped   100g butter

1 tablespoon double cream   about 300ml full-fat milk

Marinate the duck legs and breasts overnight in red wine with half the herbs. Next day, preheat the oven to 170°C/gas mark 3. Reserving the marinade, pat the duck dry and seal in a hot pan, with the skin down, over a moderate heat, so the fat is rendered. Transfer the duck to a heavy-bottomed casserole dish, removing any excess fat, cover with foil and place in the oven for 30 minutes.

Pour off half the fat in the pan and sauté the onion in the remainder. Add all the other ingredients to the casserole, including the onions, cover and return to the oven for 1 hour, or until the duck comes away from the bone easily. If the sauce becomes too thick during the cooking, thin with a little water. Ideally refrigerate and skim off any excess fat. Alternatively use kitchen paper. Preheat the oven to 180°C/gas mark 4. Remove the duck legs from the sauce. Pick the meat off the duck legs, discarding any fat in the process and return the meat to the casserole. Shred the breast meat too.

Make the mash topping: cook the potatoes and celeriac in boiling salted water until tender. Drain, mash and whisk in the butter, cream, salt and pepper and enough milk to give a thick, smooth consistency.

Transfer the meat to a pie dish and top with the mash. Bake in the preheated oven for 20 minutes or until golden and bubbling. Serve with the braised red cabbage on page 199.

Duck breasts with celeriac mash and hot cherry sauce

This was a dish developed by Leylie and Fleur for a dinner given for the Canadian ambassador to Ireland. It is relatively easy to cook and looks particularly impressive when served.

4 duck breasts

for the cherry sauce

250g stoned cherries

50g caster sugar

juice of 1 orange

1 teaspoon finely chopped shallots

2 red chillies, deseeded and finely chopped

1 glass of port

Preheat the oven to 220°C/gas mark 7. Carve a criss-cross pattern in the duck skin without cutting through to the meat. Season generously with salt and set aside for 20 minutes. Pat dry and sear, skin side down, in a medium hot pan. As the fat renders out, drain it off (this makes the best roast potatoes) but keep cooking for 5 minutes, by which time the skin should be golden and crispy.

Transfer to the preheated oven, skin side up on a baking tray, and roast for 15-25 minutes, depending on how well done you like your duck. Remove and allow to rest for at least 5 minutes in a warm place. Any juices that run from the meat can be added to your sauce.

Make the cherry sauce: combine all the ingredients in a small saucepan. Bring to the boil and simmer for 10 minutes, or until the mixture just starts to collapse.

For the celeriac mash see page 200.

Duck confit

Confit keeps almost forever, is quick to heat up - a good reason why it is so often seen on menus in south west France - and makes the most wonderful salads. Goose fat can be bought in tins from specialist shops, where it costs a fortune in comparison to the sort of price you will pay in France – a good item to stock up on when you visit.

4 duck legs
coarse sea salt
2 tablespoons fresh thyme leaves
4 garlic cloves, crushed
2 bay leaves
2 cloves
700g goose fat (enough to cover the legs completely)

Cover the duck legs with lots of sea salt and half the thyme, and leave for 24 hours. This curing draws out the moisture to give a longer shelf-life, but also introduces a texture to the meat which is an integral part of the finished dish.

Preheat the oven to 180°C/gas mark 4. Brush the salt off the duck legs and pat dry. Place the duck legs in a close-fitting saucepan. Add the remaining thyme leaves, crushed garlic, a seasoning of black pepper, the bay leaves and cloves. Cover with goose fat, cover the pan with its lid and bake in the preheated oven for 2 hours.

Remove the duck legs from the fat and allow both to cool. If you want to keep the confit, the traditional way is to place the legs in a clean pot, cover completely with the fat and allow to cool. To extract them, you heat the pot in a cool oven, just until the fat melts, extract them and roast in moderate oven, 180°C/gas mark 4, for 20 minutes, or until golden brown. Alternatively, and perhaps more practically, wrap in cling film and freeze, although they will keep quite happily in the fridge for a few days.

Serve with mash (see page 200) and braised red cabbage (see page 199). The meat, shredded, is used in a salad on page 85.

Casseroled pheasant

Most pheasant available is hung for a few days, but it is possible to hang these birds for a week, helping to make the flesh tender, moist and full of flavour.

2 pheasant
4 tablespoons olive oil
4 small leeks, trimmed and chopped
425ml chicken stock
sprig each of sage, rosemary, thyme, chopped
20 large, fat juicy white grapes
300ml cream

Preheat the oven to 200°C/gas mark 6. In an ovenproof casserole, seal the pheasant in the olive oil and season with salt and pepper.

Lay breast side up and scatter the chopped leeks around. Pour in the chicken stock, bring to the boil, add the herbs and bake, uncovered, in the preheated oven for 35 minutes.

Add the grapes and return to the oven for a further 10-15 minutes, then remove from the oven. Strain off the chicken stock (you should have about 150ml) and add the cream. If you have too much stock, reduce it down over a moderate heat or thicken with a little buerre manié.

To make a beurre manié combine an equal quantity of flour and butter, mash to a paste and stir into the sauce. For these quantities, a teaspoon of each is sufficient.

Guinea fowl and root vegetable casserole

If you not used to guinea fowl, the best way to describe it is as being similar to chicken with a slightly more robust flavour and texture, but nothing too overpowering.

1 onion, finely chopped
50g bacon lardons
2 tablespoons olive oil
4 guinea fowl breasts
2 garlic cloves
1 teaspoon chopped rosemary
1 teaspoon picked thyme leaves
1 bay leaf
2 carrots, peeled and diced
1 large parsnip, peeled and diced
2 white turnips, peeled and diced
8 peeled chestnuts
half bottle of red wine
1 teaspoon tomato purée
half 400g tin of chopped tomatoes
1 dessertspoon redcurrant jelly

Preheat the oven to 180°C/gas mark 4. In a heavy-bottomed casserole, sauté the onion and bacon in the olive oil for 10 minutes, or until lightly coloured.

Add the guinea fowl breasts, skin side down and cook for 5 minutes or until golden brown. Add the remaining ingredients and bring to a rolling boil.

Transfer to the preheated oven and bake for 30 minutes.

Variations   You can add 2 tablespoons of well rinsed Puy lentils at the same time as the garlic and herbs. This makes the dish a little more robust. If guinea fowl is hard to find, you can use corn-fed chicken.

SWEET THINGS

The urge for something sweet is hard to resist. At times it might be nothing more than a piece of chocolate, or a scoop from a tub of ice-cream, but there are plenty of instances when you want more of a celebration, when you feel like making an effort. This is the chapter for those occasions.

For a dinner party, what can be better than the fresh tangy flavour of mixed berry terrine or the richness of chocolate praline puddings. For an added celebration, why not indulge and serve with a chilled glass of dessert wine – Sauternes, a muscat, or even Sherry.

If you are hosting a supper party or buffet, the creamy delights of just-made cheesecake are hard to beat. Or consider tea time and what a difference homemade biscuits make. That uniquely consoling smell of home baking is inextricably linked with childhood.

When buying desserts has become so easy, we are often quick to forget how straightforward many of these dishes are to make yourself. Relax, make some tea and get baking.

While we sell Christmas puddings in the shops, as well as cakes and biscuits, you will find recipes for many of those items here. A chance to give in to your own passions in the comfort of your kitchen.

The desire for a little something sweet as an indulgence is as strong as ever. In an age when so much of our food is manufactured, our enthusiasm for home baking continues to grow. Good ingredients and a lightness of touch are essential

Praline

225g of shelled nuts (almonds, hazelnuts, pecans, pistachio, brazil nuts, etc.)
450g caster sugar

Lightly roast the nuts. Preheat the oven to 180°C/gas mark 4. Put the bigger nuts on one tray, the smaller on another. Cook the smaller nuts for approximately 5 minutes and the larger for 10 minutes. When ready, mix and place on a lightly oiled tray.

To make the caramel, combine the sugar and 150ml of water in a saucepan. Place on the heat and stir until the sugar dissolves. Then remove the wooden spoon and leave to boil. It will take about 10 minutes.

The colour you are looking for here is a stage darker than Golden Syrup. Remove from the heat immediately and pour over the toasted nuts. Leave to cool and break with a hammer or rolling pin and then put in a processor, depending on how fine you want it.

Chocolate praline puddings

serves 6
50g butter
350g dark chocolate (55 per cent cocoa solids)
175g caster sugar
4 eggs
few drops of vanilla extract
75g ground praline (see above)
50g plain flour

Preheat the oven to 170°C/gas mark 3 and line 6 dariole moulds with baking paper. In a bowl set over gently simmering water, melt the butter and chocolate, then stir in the sugar, eggs and vanilla. Fold in the praline and flour and mix so everything is combined.

Pour into the prepared moulds and bake in the preheated oven for about 15 minutes. The puddings will still seem soft in the middle (rather like brownies) but will continue to cook when out of the oven. Remove from the moulds while still warm. Serve with ice-cream or cream.

Raspberry and hazelnut meringue

Trying to improve on a basic meringue is no easy task, the temptation to guild the lily often too tempting. Fleur's restrained use of hazelnuts and cinnamon however, adds just the right note of interest here.

makes 9

5 egg whites
275g caster sugar
160g skinned hazelnuts, chopped
generous pinch of cinnamon
600ml whipping cream
450g fresh raspberries

Preheat the oven to 140°C/gas mark 1. On a large sheet of baking parchment drawn out 18 circles 12cm in diameter. Place the baking parchment on flat baking trays. (Do not use greaseproof as it will be difficult to remove from the meringue)

Make sure a mixing bowl is perfectly clean and dry. Place the egg whites and half the sugar in it and whisk on full power for 5-10 minutes. As the meringue forms soft peaks, begin to add the remaining caster sugar in stages. When all the sugar has been incorporated and the meringue is stiff and holding its shape, fold in 110g of the skinned, chopped hazelnuts and the cinnamon.

Spoon the mixture on to the drawn circles and spread evenly to the edges. Bake for 40 minutes, or until cooked. Remove from the oven and leave to cool on the tray. Meanwhile, toast the remaining hazelnuts.

Whip the cream so it will hold its shape when the meringues are sandwiched together. Place a meringue circle on each plate, spread over some of the cream and scatter over half the raspberries. Place the other meringue circles on top, cover with the remaining cream and raspberries. Sprinkle over the toasted hazelnuts.

Alternatively you can use the same quantities of cream and raspberries but use two 23cm meringue circles.

Mixed berries with scorched sabayon

This is a very simple dessert to do, but scores lots of marks for dramatic effect. Although it requires a little last minute preparation, everything can be left ready so it doesn't take a great deal of time. The word sabayon is borrowed from zabaglione and the concept is similar, egg yolks whisked with wine.

serves 6

900g mixed summer berries

juice of 1 lemon

25g caster sugar (depending on the sweetness of the fruit), plus more for dusting

for the sabayon

4 egg yolks

40g caster sugar

120ml white wine (light, dry or sweet)

Wash the fruit and cut any larger examples in half. Put in a bowl, sprinkle over the lemon juice, sugar and leave to macerate in the fridge for 1 hour.

To make the sabayon: whisk all the ingredients in a bowl over a pan of simmering water until doubled in volume. This will take a good 10 minutes.

To serve, place the fruits on individual heatproof plates, or one plate, spoon over the sabayon, dust with caster sugar and flash under a hot grill for a minute or two.

Little kitchen (originally jeweller's) blow torches are handy, not just for this dish, but also for crème brûlée and glazing the likes of lemon tart.

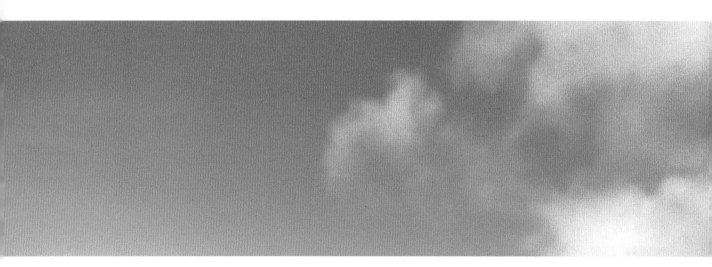

Mixed berry terrine

serves 8-10

3 heaped teaspoons powdered gelatine

200ml juice from any summer fruit

75g caster sugar

300ml sweet red lambrusco

500g mixed summer fruits, plus more to decorate

Greek yoghurt, to serve

In a bowl set over a pan of gently simmering water, dissolve the gelatine in a little of the fruit juice. Put the rest of the fruit juice and the caster sugar in a saucepan and heat gently to dissolve the sugar. Allow to cool for 5 minutes and then combine with the gelatine. Add the lambrusco.

Clean the fruit and cut any larger fruits in half or quarters. Line a 1.2 litre loaf tin with cling film, leaving some overhanging the edges. Put in half the fruit and pour over half the liquid. Place in the fridge for 1 hour, or until the mixture has set. Scatter the rest of the fruit in the tin and pour over the remaining liquid. This may have set if it got too cold. If this is the case, heat in a bowl over a saucepan of gently simmering water and pour over the fruit.

Fold over the overhanging cling film to seal. Put a flat object over the top of the tin and weigh down with two tins. Refrigerate overnight. Unwrap the cling film and turn out on to a serving plate. Decorate with fresh fruit and serve with Greek yoghurt. You need a hot sharp knife (dipped in boiling water) to cut it. Don't leave the terrine anywhere too warm for too long.

Summer pudding

The classic celebration of summer. with just a little twist here and there. Much is said about the suitablility of sliced white as the bread for summer pudding but Fleur is not inclined to agree. Go instead for something a little more special, like the brioche on page 218.

serves 8

75g sugar
50ml crème de cassis
900g mixed summer berries (redcurrants, blackcurrants, blackberries,
blueberries, raspberries and strawberries)
1 brioche loaf (see page 218)
75g apricot jam to glaze
cream, to serve

Combine the sugar, cassis and tougher berries (redcurrants, blackcurrants and blackberries) in a saucepan with 200ml water. Heat gently until the sugar has dissolved and the fruit is just soft but bright in colour. Remove from the heat and add half of the remaining fruit. Leave for 5-10 minutes then drain, reserving the syrup.

Line a 23cm loose-bottomed or springform tin with cling film. Remove the end crusts from the brioche and slice it. Line the bottom of the tin with the brioche and spoon over the fruit and enough syrup to moisten the brioche. Top with the remaining brioche. Cover the top with a base from another tin and weigh down, place in the fridge overnight. Reduce the remaining syrup to serve as a sauce.

To serve, remove the pudding from the tin and slide on to a serving plate. Top with the remaining soft fruit. Heat the apricot jam with a tablespoon of water and brush over the fruit. Serve with lots of cream and the reduced syrup. For a more elaborate finish, you can prepare individual puddings in dariole moulds. This is certainly more time-consuming, but better for serving and rather impressive.

Brioche

Rich, undoubtedly, but also delicious and ever more so when homemade. Brioche will also freeze so it might be worth considering a little batch baking. Brioche is essentially a rich, yeast-raised dough involving flour, butter and eggs.

makes two 900g loaves

450g strong white flour

pinch of salt

15g dried yeast

50g caster sugar

50ml warm water

4 eggs

225g unsalted butter

egg wash, to glaze

The day before sieve the flour and salt into a bowl. Dissolve the yeast and sugar in the warm water. Put the flour, yeast and eggs into a food mixer. Using the dough hook, mix to a stiff smooth paste. Then gradually add the butter, small amounts at a time. This will take roughly 15 minutes. When finished it should have a silky appearance. Place in an oiled bowl and leave to rise overnight in the fridge.

The next day, preheat the oven to 170°C/gas mark 3. Knead the dough lightly, divide in two and place in the loaf tins. Brush with egg wash and leave to rise until doubled in size. Egg-wash again and bake for 30-40 minutes until cooked (a skewer inserted into the centre should come out clean).

Bread and butter pudding

Bread and butter pudding was traditionally made to use up stale bread with milk, eggs and a few raisins thrown in for a bit of luxury. Hilary Pratt decided on brioche during a holiday in France, where sliced bread is harder to come by. The end result was rather sensational.

serves 6-8

2 loaves brioche (see opposite)

50g softened butter

8 egg yolks

175g caster sugar, plus a little more

1 vanilla pod, split

300ml milk

300ml cream

fresh pouring cream, to serve

Discard the ends of the brioche and cut into slices. Butter these and then cut in half. Arrange the slices in a shallow (1.75 litre) dish. Beat the egg yolks with the caster sugar. Place the split vanilla pod in a saucepan with the milk and cream and gently bring to a simmer. Pour on to the egg yolks and sugar mixture, stirring briskly. Pour over the buttered brioche and leave aside for 30 minutes to allow the brioche to absorb the flavours. Preheat the oven to 180°C/gas mark 4.

Place the dish in a roasting tin and pour boiling water into the roasting tin so it comes three quraters of the way up the side. Cover the pudding lightly with foil and bake for 30 minutes, or until the pudding begins to set. Remove the foil for the last 10 minutes.

Remove the pudding from the roasting tin, sprinkle generously with caster sugar and brown under a grill. If brioche is hard to come by, or you are short of time, panettone is a good substitute

Lavender and rosemary roast plums with lime mascarpone

6 plums
4 stalks of lavender or rosemary
50g light brown sugar
1 dessertspoon brandy

for the mascarpone cream
225g mascarpone
1 dessert spoon icing sugar
finely shredded zest of 2 limes

100ml honey, warmed

Preheat the oven to 180°C/gas mark 4. Halve and stone the plums, and thread on to the lavender or rosemary stalks. Cover the ends with tin foil to prevent them burning. Sprinkle with the light brown sugar and brandy and roast in the preheated oven, for 15-20 minutes. You want them to hold their shape.

To make the mascarpone cream, simply mix the mascarpone, icing sugar and lime zest.

Serve the plums warm, with the mascarpone cream spooned into each plum half. Drizzle over the honey.

Favourite plum varieties include the fairly common Victoria as well as the likes of Early Laxtons, Pershore Yellow Eggs and Warwickshire Drooper. Look for soft, heavy fruit with deep colouring.

Chocolate chip cookies

makes about 14

225g butter

225g caster sugar

1 egg yolk

1-2 drops vanilla extract

250g plain flour

$^1/_2$ level teaspoon bread soda

125g milk chocolate drops

125g dark chocolate drops

Cream the butter and sugar, then add in the egg yolk and vanilla extract. Sieve in the flour and bread soda, then mix in the chocolate. Shape into a long thin cylinder, wrap in cling film and leave in the fridge for 1 hour. Preheat the oven to 170°C/gas mark 3. Cut the dough cylinder into slices and place on a lined baking sheet. Cook for 20-25 minutes.

Spices

Toasting spices is one of the most glorious of kitchen tasks, the room filling with the heady scent of cumin and coriander, saffron and star anise, cinnamon and cardamom pods.

We tend to associate spices with the cooking of the East, yet we have been using them for centuries – in baking, in stews and casseroles and in soups. Historically expensive, their use was consequently limited. Perhaps it is this which lends them such a special air, a kind of otherworldly quality. What is not in doubt, however, is how much they can add to a dish. Used sparingly, yet with confidence, these powerful ingredients will transform your food from the everyday to the exotic.

Nutmeg and mace
Mace is the lacy aril which surrounds the seed, nutmeg is the kernel. Both have a rich, warm aroma, the taste bordering on medicinal. Widely used in both sweet and savoury dishes, both spices go well with veal, potatoes and pasta as well as sweets, biscuits and cream cheese.

Cinnamon
Cinnamon has a spicy butteriness, with a hint of wood smoke and should smell sweetly. It is one of those spices equally at home in sweet and savoury foods. Great with lamb, perfect with rice, a star in fruit salad, it shines with chocolate.

Coriander seed
Mildly sweet, with a burning, orange-peel flavour that is subtle, but full-bodied. In the Middle East coriander seed is particularly popular with lamb.

Star anise
Providing a warm, sharp licorice flavour, this is a key ingredient in Chinese five-spice powder. It is also used in Vietnamese cuisine and is particularly good with fish and poultry.

Cardamom
This has a lemony, citrus, jewel-like flavour, almost like rose-water and is delicate, but searingly penetrating. Widely used in both sweet and savoury dishes, green cardamoms are considered the best, as white cardamoms are blanched and less powerful.

Cloves
Nibble a clove and you are in for a shock - it is sharp, fiery and bitter, with a fair chilli-whack of heat. Cook it, however, and these characteristics become much more subdued, although it retains a dark, rich assertive flavour.

Cumin seed
With its strong, long-lasting, slightly bitter flavour, cumin has a warm, approachable character, extenuated when it is dry-roasted.

Pink peppercorns
These are not really peppercorns at all, being the soft berry of the Schinus tere-binthifolius, with a flavour that is somewhat resinous.

From left to right: cumin, mace, cloves, pink peppercorns, star anis, cinnamon sticks, cardamom pods, nutmeg

Cinnamon buns

makes 8

450g strong white flour

pinch of salt

50g caster sugar

50g butter

200ml milk

25g dried yeast

1 egg, plus extra to egg-wash

for the filling

100g unsalted butter

100g light golden brown sugar

1 teaspoons ground cinnamon

1 egg, beaten

Sieve the flour, salt and sugar into a bowl, then rub in the butter. Heat the milk to blood temperature and pour into a bowl with the yeast. Mix in the egg. Combine the two mixtures (using the dough hook or by hand) until springy and smooth. Put into an oiled bowl, cover with cling film and leave to rise for 30 minutes to one hour, the time taken depending on the warmth of the surroundings. Knock the dough back and knead lightly. Combine all the ingredients for the filling and mix together with a wooden spoon.

Roll out a quarter of the dough and use to line the base of a 23cm cake tin. Roll the rest out into a large rectangular shape and spread with the cinnamon filling. Egg-wash the longer edge and roll the dough up towards this. You should finish with a long thin cylindrical shape. Cut this into 8 slices .

Egg-wash the dough lining the tin. Place the slices with the pinwheel effect showing on the egg-washed dough. Egg-wash the top and leave somewhere warm to rise for 30-40 minutes.

Preheat the oven to 180°C/gas mark 4. Egg-wash the top again and sprinkle with light golden brown sugar. Bake for 30 minutes, or until cooked through.

Lemon curd cake

You may not need all the curd, but it keeps in the fridge for about two weeks and is delicious on toast.

serves 8-10

225g butter, plus more for greasing

225g caster sugar

4 eggs

225g self-raising flour, sieved

grated zest of 1 lemon and juice of half, plus more zest to decorate

for the lemon curd

grated zest and juice of 5-6 lemons   225g unsalted butter, diced   275g caster sugar   10 eggs, lightly beaten

for the lemon butter icing

50g butter, softened   50g icing sugar   1 teaspoon lemon juice

for the glacé icing

275g icing sugar   lemon juice (whatever you have left from the half lemon, with water if necessary to mix)

Preheat the oven to 170°C/gas mark 3. Butter a 23cm springform tin and line it with baking paper. Cream the butter and sugar until light and fluffy. Add the eggs gradually, alternating with the flour, then add the lemon zest and juice. Place in the prepared tin and bake for 55 minutes to 1 hour. Remove from the oven and leave to cool on a wire rack.

Make the lemon curd: put the lemon zest and juice, butter and caster sugar in a bowl over a saucepan of simmering water, making sure the bowl does not touch the water. Stir occasionally until the butter has melted and the sugar dissolved. Stir in the eggs and leave for 40 minutes to one hour, stirring occasionally. The curd is ready when it coats the back of the wooden spoon. Remove from the heat, leave to cool and then refrigerate.

Make the lemon butter icing by putting all ingredients in a bowl and beating until light and fluffy. Make the glacé icing by mixing the ingredients in a bowl. To decorate the cake, cut a thin layer out of the top of it and whizz this in a food processor to crumbs, then place on a tray in the oven preheated to 150°C/gas mark 2 for 5 minutes to toast.

Cut the cake across into three discs and sandwich with lemon curd. Refrigerate for an hour to firm up. Cover the side of the cake with the butter icing and roll the cake in the toasted cake crumbs. Cover the top of the cake in glacé icing and decorate with lemon zest.

Pecan and maple streusel cheesecake

serves 6-8

225g shortbread biscuits

35g unsalted butter (less if the shortbread biscuits are homemade), plus more for greasing

625g cream cheese

225g light golden brown sugar

3 eggs

125ml whipping cream

1 teaspoon natural vanilla extract or 1 vanilla pod (scraped)

for the streusel topping

25g butter   50g pecans, roughly chopped   75g shortbread biscuits, crumbled, but still with texture

25g light golden brown sugar

for the maple sauce

35g butter   50g caster sugar   75ml maple syrup   125ml cream

Preheat the oven to 140°C/gas mark 1. Butter a 23cm springform cake tin and line it with baking paper.

Crush the shortbread (the quickest way is between 2 sheets of greaseproof paper using a rolling pin). Melt the butter, mix the shortbread with it and sprinkle it over the base of the prepared tin.

Beat the cream cheese and sugar together, then gradually beat in the eggs. Stir in the cream and vanilla extract. Pour over the biscuit base and bake for 50 minutes to one hour. It should still have a slight wobble when cooked and it may have cracked; don't worry, the streusel topping covers a lot.

To make the streusel topping: in a non-stick frying pan, melt the butter over a low heat. Add the pecans and cook gently for 1-2 minutes. Add the crumbled shortbread and sugar, and cook for another 2-3 minutes, stirring frequently. Leave to cool slightly and then pour over the cake. Allow to cool to room temperature.

To make the maple sauce: put all the ingredients in a saucepan and bring slowly to the boil. Cook until the mixture has become a light caramel colour, about 5 minutes. Serve with the cheesecake.

Triple-layer chocolate truffle cake

serves 12

4 small eggs

100g caster sugar

75g self-raising flour

25g cocoa

for the syrup

75ml milk   20ml brandy   20ml honey

for the fillings

110g chocolate (70 per cent cocoa solids), melted with 50ml of cream   225g white chocolate, melted with 50ml of cream 500ml double or whipping cream, lightly whipped

for the icing

350g milk chocolate   75ml whipping cream

Preheat the oven to 180°C/gas mark 4. Grease and line a 23cm springform cake tin. Whisk the eggs and sugar until thick, which will take about 10 minutes. Sieve the flour and cocoa and fold into the egg mixture. Spoon into the prepared cake tin and bake for 20-25 minutes, or until cooked. Remove from the oven and leave to cool on a wire rack.

To make the syrup: put all the ingredients in a saucepan and heat gently until combined. Do not boil.

Remove the cake from the tin and line the tin with cling film. (Make sure you use enough cling film to cover the cake completely). Cut the cake across its depth into 2 halves. Place half the cake back in the lined tin and brush with the syrup.

Make the fillings by combining each of the melted chocolate mixtures with half the whipped cream. Spoon half the white chocolate mixture over the bottom half of the cake. Follow with the dark chocolate mixture. Finish with the remaining white chocolate mixture. Brush the other half of the cake with the syrup and place on top. Cover the cake with the cling film and place in the fridge to set overnight.

Combine the milk choclate and cream and heat gently to melt. Remove the cake from the tin and spread the chocolate icing over the top and sides.

Liz Orr's tea brack

An Irish favourite and a must with a cup of tea in the afternoon on a wet day. This recipe was given to Leylie by a late neighbour and has been treasured ever since. Quite what the secret ingredient is has yet to be discovered, but the quest means lots of hours of baking and many happy memories.

makes 3x 900g loaves

450g dark brown sugar

2^{1}/2 cups of tea

half cup whiskey

450g sultanas

450g mixed fruit

3 eggs

450g plain flour

3 teaspoons baking powder

3 teaspoons mixed spice

honey, for glazing

Dissolve the sugar in the tea, mix in the whiskey and soak the fruit overnight in this. Next day, preheat the oven to 170°C/gas mark 3 and line 3 loaf tins with greaseproof paper. Mix the eggs, flour, baking powder and mixed spice with the fruit mixture and pour into the prepared tins. Bake for 1 hour. Test with a skewer, which should come out clean. Remove from the oven and brush with honey. To make your honey runny, place the jar in a bowl of boiling water for 5 minutes.

Mince pies

makes 9

275g unsalted butter, cubed

450g plain flour

75g ground almonds

50g icing sugar

2 egg yolks

20-30ml milk to bind

for the mincemeat

2 apples, grated

grated zest and juice of 2 lemons

450g vegetarian suet

110g mixed peel

2 tablespoons marmalade

225g currants

450g raisins

225g sultanas

900g dark brown sugar

125ml whiskey

Combine the flour, almonds and sugar. Rub in the butter so the mixture looks like breadcrumbs. Make a well in the centre and add the egg yolks. Stir gently, adding enough milk to form a dough. Cover with cling film and refrigerate.

At least the day before, make the mincemeat by combining all the ingredients in a bowl. Stir well, cover with a cloth and set aside overnight.

Preheat the oven to 200°C/gas mark 6. Roll out the pastry to about 3mm thick and cut nine 7.5cm rounds using a pastry cutter. Roll up the scraps with the remaining pastry, roll out again and cut nine 6cm circles. You can then cut or decorate them as in the photograph.

Grease the mince pie tins well and gently line them with the larger circles. Fill with mincemeat so they are just full. Dampen the edges with water and top with the smaller discs, then firmly pinch them to seal. For any that you have not cut holes, snip with scissors to allow the air to escape.

Brush lightly with milk and bake in the preheated oven for 30 minutes, or until golden brown. Allow to cool and sprinkle with sugar.

Granny Doupe's Christmas puddings

The secret to a good Christmas pudding lies as much in the time it is allowed to mature as the mixture. Make up to two months in advance and serve with brandy butter and whipped cream.

makes 4 x 450g puddings

450g sultanas

450g currants

450g raisins

110g glacé cherries (halved)

450g brown sugar

275g breadcrumbs

275g self-raising flour

2 teaspoons mixed spice

1 teaspoon freshly grated nutmeg

225g nibbed almonds

110g mixed peel (whole peel chopped)

350g butter, melted

6 eggs

grated zest and juice of 2 oranges

1 small can of Guinness

a little milk (optional)

2 tablespoons whiskey

Wash the sultanas, currants, raisins and cherries. Place the sugar, breadcrumbs, flour, spices, almonds and mixed peel in a large bowl and mix well. Melt the butter and beat the eggs lightly. Add the butter, eggs, orange juice and zest and Guinness to the dry mix and stir thoroughly. If the mixture seems a little dry, moisten with milk.

Spoon into four 450g pudding bowls and cover with a lid. If using delph bowls, place a double piece of parchment paper over the bowl, followed by a double piece of tin foil and tie down with string. Steam for 4-5 hours, then leave the pudding to go cold. Remove the lid and wash it. Spray the pudding with whiskey and cover with the clean lid.

On Christmas Day, place the pudding in a pot on a raised metal ring (like a large cutter) and pour in enough boiling water to reach $2/3$ up the sides of the pudding basin. Simmer over a gentle heat for 1.5 hours making sure it does not boil dry.

Edible gifts

In the Avoca shops we are trying all the time to create more and more edible gifts, particularly at Christmas when there seems to be an increasing move towards artisan presents. Many of these kinds of gifts can also be made at home. They need not be complicated, or even that time-consuming, although the vehicles for delivery may need a little advance thought. This may be nothing more than tissue paper in a box, a kilner jar wrapped with some raffia, or a basket, but these little touches make all the difference. What follows are a few suggestions of gifts that are easy and fun to make, so simple that children can join in too.

Truffles   *makes about 30-40*   **300ml double or whipping cream   450g dark chocolate (55 per cent cocoa solids), broken into bite-sized pieces   50g unsalted butter   50ml brandy   cocoa powder, for dusting**

In a small pan, heat the cream until almost boiling. Remove from the heat and pour over the chocolate, butter and brandy. Whisk to ensure everything is melted, pour into a roasting tin and allow to cool to room temperature. Transfer to the fridge and leave overnight.

Using a teaspoon or melon baller, form into balls and drop into a bowl of cocoa powder. Roll so they are coated in the powder and then refrigerate. Serve on a white or glass plate, or pack in tissue paper as a gift. You can give chocolate truffles that smooth glossy finish by tempering chocolate. This involves melting it, cooling it and then reheating it again. The process is long-winded and requires a practiced hand, which is why we have given the cocoa covering here.

Chocolate-covered orange peel   *makes about 350g*   **110g dark chocolate (55% cocoa solids), broken into bite-sized pieces   1 teaspoon unsalted butter   225g candied orange peel, thinly sliced**

Combine the chocolate and butter in a bowl and melt over a pan of simmering water. Dip the orange peel in the melted chocolate so they are half covered. Lay on greaseproof paper to set in a cool place.

Preserved lemons   *makes about 6*   **16 lemons   sea salt**

Cut six of the lemons vertically but not quite through to the base. Stuff sea salt into the cut sides and place in a sterilised kilner jar. Squeeze the remaining lemons and pour the juice into the jar. Seal and leave for a couple of weeks before using.

DELIMONGERING

For most of us, cooking starts with shopping. The lucky few will pick vegetables from their garden, pluck apples from their orchards, haul fish from the sea or shoot their own game. But for the majority of people, a trip down the high street is a prerequisite.

Shopping needs to approximate these experiences as closely as possible, we need to get as close to the source as we can. A lettuce picked hours ago will be full of vitality. Fish that hits the fishmongers slab within hours of being caught delivers a totally different experience to one eaten days later. Peaches picked in the warm summer sun deliver bags more flavour than those picked before they are ripe so they are robust enough to travel.

The skill of retailing well requires great knowledge, attention to detail and time, the kinds of attributes found in small retailers whose relationship is partly with their raw ingredients and partly with their customers. If you are a regular, take time to communicate, praise and criticize, you can influence and learn. The process becomes two-way. Change is constant; what exists today in limited quantity will be widely available tomorrow.

What follows is a listing of items that all too often end up being considered and bought as commodities, when the artisan and small-scale producers deliver so much more in terms of taste and texture. Although generally more expensive, the difference is often marginal between an international brand and something made with love, care and attention by a family run business.

Cheese   Cheese in general develops with age, but does so in an uneven manner requiring skill and practice. The right temperature and humidity are crucial. In France the person who ages cheese, who brings them on, is known as an affineur, and they can transform a cheese from being simply nice to being sensational.

Not all delicatessens know how to bring cheese on and if you are lucky to live near a specialist cheese retailer they are well worth cultivating. If you are not so lucky, there is good news, most will mail your order so it is with you the next day, along with instructions for keeping.

Cheese retailers to consider: *Sheridan's* (in Dublin at their shop and Temple Bar Market, Galway)
Cheeses we use in the cafés and sell in the Foodhalls: *Gubben, Cashel Blue, Old Shropshire, Durrus, Roquefort, Manchego, Pecorino de Pienza secca, Crottin de Chavignol, Parmegiano Reggiano, Montgomery Cheddar, Colston Bassett Stilton, Vintage Doolin*

Jams and preserves   A plethora of companies have been established in Ireland over the last few years producing jams, preserves, chutneys and relishes. Some of those listed below we stock, others are to be found in independent outlets throughout the country. In general we look for a high fruit and vegetable content and minimal preservatives – as close to homemade as we can get.

Brands to look out for include: *Avoca Pantry, the Bay Tree Food Company, Filligans, Crossogue*

Italian jarred products   These include pesto sauces, bagna cauda, roasted peppers and a whole range of antipasti, from stuffed peppers to grilled scallions.

Brands to look out for include: *Mongetto, the Delize Italiane range, Crossogue*

Olive oil   There are a huge number of oils on sale, so many it is often hard to distinguish one from another. The most important aspect to choosing an olive oil is finding the one you like. Tuscan oils appeal to some for their strong, peppery flavours; others like the elegance of French olive oil. As a general rule, the further south you go, the more fiery, grassy and herbaceous olive oil becomes.

Acidity is what makes olive oil taste bitter and unpleasant. The higher the acidity the more fatty the oil will taste in the mouth. Low acidity gives it a smooth silkiness. Olive oil is graded on this basis - along with other factors, like whether it actually tastes very nice – as well as how the oil is extracted from the olive. Spain, it is worth noting, has a system for grading extra virgin olive oil similar to that used in many European countries to grade wine. Store olive oil in a cool dark place, sunlight is to be avoided.

Brands to look out for: *Roi, Frateli Pinna, Mancianti, Ravida, Iliada, Carluccio's Ligurian, Nunez de Prado, Carbonell, Alziari, The Fresh Olive Oil company own label, Olives et Al Hojiblanca, Tesco Extra Virgin*

Pasta   This storecupboard stable may seem so straightforward and basic there hardly seems much one can say about it. But this would be far from the truth. Dried supermarket pasta used to be terrible, indeed some of it still is. The better examples are manufactured by one or other of the large Italian companies.

Still, the recipe gets tweaked to fit perceived expectations, in terms of taste and texture, as well as price constraints. Time is also a important and that too, costs money. Industrially made pasta is combined in vast quantities, yet the kneading can be fast or slow and can take place at high or low temperatures, all of which influnce the final result. It is then pushed through a die cast in the required shape. These can be made from metal or from super-smooth Teflon, the latter a faster, but less satisfactory method.

Finally and perhaps most importantly is the drying. Done at speed, the end result can lack body and substance, while pasta that is dried slowly tends more closely to resemble the dry natural conditions of a southern Italian farmhouse baking in midday sun.

Brands to look out for include: the mass-market but excellent *De Cecco* and *Barilla*, both used extensively in restaurants. Others to consider include *Giovani Perna, Benedetto Cavalieri, Carluccio's*

Balsamic and other vinegars

A few years ago nobody had heard of balsamic vinegar, these days it is hard to get away from it. Real balsamic vinegar (look for 'tradizionale' on the label) is expensive, requiring at least 10 years aging and often the better brands have been aged for a great deal more. Other aceto balsamicos can be good, but are not aged for as long. With the growth in enthusiasm for balsamico other

sweet-and-sour vinegars have come on the market and there has been renewed interest in the likes of sherry vinegar. Vinegars are a great way to make subtle changes, in vinaigrettes for example, or when used to deglaze pans. A good vinegar can do wonders when sparingly sprinkled on stawberries or incorporated into vanilla ice-cream. If you think these vinegars are expensive consider how long a bottle will last, months if not years and what a wealth of variety they offer the cook.

Brands to look out for: *Forum, Valdespino, Bonissima*

Smoked foods and cured meats   The last few years have seen several new smokeries start up. Too often the tendency is to try and smoke everything under the sun, not always with much success. The following have concentrated on a limited range, put their energies into the smoking rather than the gimmicks.

Brands to look out for include: *Woodcock Smokery, Rannoch Smokery, Gubben Smokehouse, Hederman, Ummera, Kinvara, Rudd's*

Tinned and jarred pulses, anchovies, sardines and tuna fish   Tinned goods have something of a tarnished image, akin to frozen food, they are seen as a commodity, much of a muchness. This may be true of the international brands, but not if you focus on the smaller companies. Typically these are Spanish, Italian, Portuguese and French.

Brands to look out for include: *Metelliana, Marie Elisabeth, Conservas Alegria, Ortiz, Bunalun.*

Coffee   Real coffee is as complex and sophisticated as wine, so it's no wonder similar terms are used to describe its taste: acid, bitter, sweet, rich, mellow, smooth, even gamey. So much for meaningless phrases like 'breakfast blend'. If you needed only one reason to go to a speciality retailer, it might be to get an accurate description of what you are buying. Price differentials are nothing like as dramatic as you might imagine.

Brands to consider include: *Illy, Lavazza* and an organic coffee we sell in the shops, *Caffe Nativo.*

Chocolate   The percentage of cocoa solids is a good indicator of the quality of chocolate, but not a guarantee. Around 60 per cent is considered good, 70 per cent even better. More than that, and the bitterness can be too powerful for some, a bit like a double-strength espresso. The better brands tend to be French and Belgian, and some of the better supermarket own-brands will be made in these countries.

Brands to look out for include *Valrhona* and *Callebaut*

Spices   The best advice is to buy from ethnic stores, both the owners and customers tend to know what they are talking about. This advice holds throughout Europe. Turnover is high, ensuring freshness, customers are a discriminating bunch and most of the spices sold are whole. The neat rows of glass jars in supermarkets may look pretty, but some of them have been there for quite some time.

SUPPLIERS

Throughout this book reference is made to the growing band of small Irish artisan food producers. Many if not most have been uncovered in *The Bridgestone Food Lovers Guide to Ireland* by John and Sally McKenna. This terrific book lists in glorious detail every hole in the hedge worth investigating. Their style is upbeat, if they don't like something it will be conspicuously absent until it is worth a mention. Keep a copy in your glove box and explore the best that Ireland has to offer.

We are witnessing a dramatic change in how we have come to see food in Ireland. Where once someone producing cheese, brown bread, or jam, a smoked salmon or a few eggs at the farm gate was seen as being rather odd, these days they are admired and in fact they should be revered. It is only by buying this produce that it will survive; it is an important part of our heritage. If we want to see sales of local produce at the farm gate, in small delis and enjoy country markets we have to participate if they are to prosper. We will all be richer for the success of our artisan food culture. You only have to look to the culture of France and Italy to see how well this works. If we only shop in supermarkets, supermarkets will be all there is. And what if you cleared a few square metres of space in your own garden? Rocket will grow like a weed under a sheet of glass while tomatoes picked fresh and warm are a delight to the senses and one of the most evocative of memories. New Irish potatoes loosened by your own fork, steamed and served with butter and mint are a marvel. Parsley will run riot. A few hens running around will eat vegetable scraps and deliver yellow yolks only seen in the freshest eggs. Who knows where it all might end!

Even with a window box there is no reason not to grow herbs, one of the 'secret' ingredients of many cooks. Used delicately, herbs lift and add body to so many savoury dishes. Cut freshly, chives add bite, chervil style and basil the kind of heady glorious aroma that can only be linked with summer and fresh tomatoes.

Time to don the gloves and get digging.

Simon Pratt

INDEX

Acknowledgements

The idea for a second Avoca Café Cookbook was hatched during the last days of 2001 when Simon Pratt approached me with the observation that Avoca had many more recipes to offer and maybe some sound advice. Where in the first book we had told the story of Avoca the second book was to take the far less tangible, but nonetheless real, aspects of quality, attention to detail, freshness, skill, knowledge and most of all passion and share them with a wider audience. Avoca is about aiming for excellence, he said, and we should try to make that available to others.

Like all good ideas however, this came with a caveat, the book needed to be published in time for Christmas 2002. A tall order by any standards, but it is to Simon's credit that he firmly believed it could be done.

This book was to evolve from book one, but more a stage further and to achieve that the same team was assembled.

My thanks, admiration and gratitude go to Leylie Hayes, Fleur Campbell and Eimer Rainsford. Leylie Hayes now looks after five kitchens and has scores of chefs looking to her for leadership and guidance. That she does it with such charm – more than the odd sharply observed witticism – and professionalism leaves me in awe. Both Eimer and Fleur cooked, styled and laughed their way through weeks of shooting with a style, wit and charm that kept us all, too often, dumbstruck. A special thanks to Teresa Byrne the superlative general manager of the Avoca Cafes. For everyone else at Avoca my thanks for the endless cups of tea, delicious lunches and never ending smiles.

Vanessa Courtier has once again grasped both pictures and text with both hands and fashioned a whole from many disparate parts. Moving to a second book, making it different and at the same time similar to the first is never easy, but the result is as amazing as it is expected, yet again!

Georgia Glynn Smith's canny eye for the angle, her refreshing ability to look at a plate of food with her inherent sense of humour continues to inspire.

The recipes were shot at Powerscourt and at Leylie Hayes's home in County Wicklow during the spring of 2002. Other photographs were taken in Dublin and around County Wicklow at the same time. A special thank you to Marc Michel for allowing us to photograph on his farm in Kilpedder, Co Wicklow. His produce appears in a number of photographs and we are grateful for his cooperation.

Hugo Arnold